More Strange Tales
of the Civil War

By

Michael Sanders

BURD STREET PRESS
SHIPPENSBURG, PENNSYLVANIA

This Burd Street Press publication
was printed by
Beidel Printing House, Inc.
63 West Burd Street
Shippensburg, PA 17257-0708 USA

The acid-free paper used in this book meets the guidelines for permanence and durability of the Committee on Production Guidelines for Book Longevity of the Council on Library Resources.

For a complete list of available publications
please write
Burd Street Press
Division of White Mane Publishing Company, Inc.
P.O. Box 708
Shippensburg, PA 17257-0708 USA

ISBN-10: 1-57249-383-6
ISBN-13: 978-1-57249-383-4

Library of Congress Cataloging-in-Publication Data

Sanders, Michael, 1961-
    More strange tales of the Civil War / by Michael Sanders.
        p. cm.
    Includes bibliographical references and index.
    ISBN-13: 978-1-57249-383-4 ISBN-10: 1-57249-383-6 (alk. paper)
    1. United States--History--Civil War, 1861-1865--Anecdotes. 2. Curiosities and wonders--Anecdotes.

E655.S25 2006
973.7--dc22

                                                                    2006042509

PRINTED IN THE UNITED STATES OF AMERICA

Contents

Illustrations

Acknowledgments

A book is seldom written without the aid and support of many people. *More Strange Tales of the Civil War* is no exception.

Many hours are spent poring over resources to acquire the information necessary to complete each story. Just acquiring these resources takes the help and patience of many individuals. First and foremost is the staff at the United States Army Military History Institute at the Carlisle Barracks. Without their help and the Institute's resources this book would have been much more difficult to write. Scott Hartwig of the Gettysburg National Battlefield Park helped in acquiring information on the death of Colonel Edward Cross. In addition the staffs of the Penn State University Patee Library, Bucknell University Betrand Library, and the Herr Memorial Library of Mifflinburg provided resources at critical times in the writing process.

In the quest for illustrations I am indebted to Sidney Dreese. Sidney aided in selecting illustrations and used his knowledge to help photograph them.

The staff at White Mane Publishing deserves a great deal of credit for their patience and enthusiasm for publishing my first volume, *Strange Tales of the Civil War*. In doing so they gave me the chance I needed to be successful with that book. By putting out such a great product they helped to lay the foundation for this volume.

Most importantly I would like to acknowledge the love and support of my wife, Bronwen. As a fellow historian she is a sounding board for various ideas and served as an editor while producing this work. In addition, during the course of the writing process she has given me the greatest gift of all, a son. As I write this, Owen is now fifteen months old and very much into exploring his world. It is Owen who makes everything worthwhile and so much more fun and challenging.

Introduction

People are drawn to the unusual. Even in our ordinary lives we are inundated with odd things. When visiting a mall or walking down a busy street we are quick to observe anything unusual about a person. How they look or how they walk. By scanning the channels on television we have the opportunity to view a host of shows dealing with strange events, haunted places, and odd people. I include myself as one of those curious people who are fascinated by anything considered to be odd. It is that fascination and my lifelong interest in the Civil War that led me to research and write the first volume, *Strange Tales of the Civil War*. The success of that first book prompted me to begin researching and writing a second volume.

Like the first book, this volume is filled with short stories dealing with men and women who lived through the most terrifying period in America history—a time when our country was literally tearing itself apart. They all have a story to tell of their experiences during this time. I have researched and found some stories that can be considered bizarre or strange. These tales are recorded, many times by the people that experienced them. They are found in regimental histories, newspapers, and veteran magazines. Some of the names are of the famous, but many are ordinary people caught up in the turmoil of the time.

As a teacher of history I have found that students perk up when they hear a somewhat strange story of some episode in history. I hope readers will find these stories as interesting to read as they were to research and write.

Chapter One

Animal Curiosities

Sallie's Premonition

The old saying is "dogs are man's best friend," and so when the men went to war so did their canine companions. It is little wonder that they would be looked upon with so much favor. Young men, away from home, many for the first time, would no doubt become homesick. A good remedy for this ailment is a dog, a little reminder of the innocence of home. These dogs quickly became favorites of the men, who turned them into regimental mascots. Frequently they are mentioned in Civil War literature, and even during regimental reunions these canine warriors had a front seat when a picture was taken for posterity.

One of the most famous mascots of the Civil War was a brindle bull terrier named Sallie Ann Jarrett or Sallie for short. Sallie was the mascot of the 11th Pennsylvania Volunteers, joining the regiment as a puppy at Camp Wayne near West Chester, Pennsylvania.[1] It didn't take long for Sallie to become a favorite of the men. "She knew the roll of the drum at reveille, was out of quarters among the first, and regularly attended the morning roll-call." When the 11th was on the march, Sallie was with them running alongside the men.[2]

It was at the Battle of Gettysburg where Sallie won lasting fame. During the morning of the first day the 11th was positioned along McPhearson's Ridge. Around noontime the men were forced to retreat with the rest of the Union line back through the town of Gettysburg to Cemetery Hill. Instead of fleeing, Sallie remained with the dead and wounded of the 11th on the ridge. For two more days the battle raged, but Sallie remained in her position, which was now behind Confederate lines.

It wasn't until July 4 that relief finally came when the Confederate army retreated south and Union troops reoccupied McPhearson's Ridge. Sallie was quick to recognize the blue-clad soldiers of the North, especially men of the 11th Pennsylvania. It was reported that Sallie was "weak and emaciated from the enforced fast," but being among friends once again she was quick to regain her health.[3]

The following May the 11th Pennsylvania participated in the Battle of the Wilderness. During this engagement Sallie was wounded in the neck. A surgeon inspected the wound but was unable to remove the ball. Sallie returned to the regiment and carried the ball for several months until it finally fell out by its own accord.

Between marching and fighting, Sallie was able to pursue other activities such as rabbit chasing, napping, and even motherhood. During the war Sallie bore several litters of puppies, much to the delight of the men. But she always returned to her duties as mascot of the regiment.[4]

Sadly though, Sallie's days, like many of her companions' in blue, were numbered. Whether Sallie understood the dangers of battle can never be known. However, the men of the 11th were convinced that she had some type of feeling that darkness was soon to fall upon her life. The night of February 5, 1865, Sallie quartered with several men of Company D. She was usually welcomed wherever she chose to sleep. However, during this particular evening her welcome grew thin. Sometime during the night the men were awakened by mournful cries from Sallie. She was checked for injuries but none were found. The men tried to return to their sleep but Sallie persisted with her crying. Becoming agitated, the groggy men tried to drive her from the tent, but to no avail. She simply returned to issue forth the same cries of agony.

The next morning the 11th marched to Hatcher's Run near Petersburg, Virginia. Sallie ran, as usual, at the head of the column. The 11th almost immediately went into battle. Sallie was in line with the file closers during the first assault when she was hit in the head and killed instantly. One of the members of the 11th wrote, "Poor Sallie fell in the front line in the fight at the Run—a bullet pierced her brain. She was buried where she fell by some of the boys, even while under a murderous enemy fire."[5]

The survivors of the 11th Pennsylvania Volunteers ensured that Sallie would be forever remembered. When they erected their monument to the fallen heroes of Gettysburg, a statue of Sallie was placed at its base to commemorate her role in the battle and the regiment's history.

The Hogs of Gettysburg

Hogs. To the Civil War soldier, like men in all wars, the word *hog* meant food: ham, ribs, and sausage. There are many instances in memoirs and regimental histories where a stray hog wandered into camp to be a special guest at the supper table. However, on the second night during the Battle of Gettysburg the tables were turned.

The fighting in and around the Wheatfield at Gettysburg was horrific. So much blood was shed in this area that it's been called the whirlpool of the battle. By the time the second day of fighting was complete, this twenty-six-acre field had changed hands six times. In human blood it equaled 6,955 men who were reported as killed, wounded, or missing.[6]

That night the field was alive with men screaming and others moaning in pain. Blood and its scent was everywhere. Then, as if man's inhumanity to man wasn't enough, another agony slowly emerged onto the field—an agony possibly more hideous than the fighting earlier in the day. There in the dark of the night wandered several hogs. They were likely from a nearby farm where fences were broken, freeing the creatures. Happenstance brought them to this area of the battlefield. Unfortunately for the wounded this was a serious situation. Hogs are drawn to the scent of blood and will eat meat without regard of where it comes from. In addition full-grown hogs weighing several hundred pounds are very dangerous animals, especially if threatened or excited. Their protruding tusks can easily tear flesh.

That night as the hogs wandered into the Wheatfield, they began to graze on the grass. Slowly their distant grunting could be heard as they grew closer to the wounded men. Once in a while they emitted squeals that could raise the hair on the back of a person's neck. But slowly they lumbered on and fed.

Lieutenant Barzilia Inman of Company F, 118th Pennsylvania Volunteers, was wounded during the day's fighting.[7]

He later recalled his terrifying ordeal with the hogs that night in the Wheatfield:

> That night a number of stray hogs came to where I lay and commenced rooting and tearing at the dead men around me. Finally one fellow that in the darkness looked of enormous size approached and attempted to poke me—grunting loudly the while. Several others also came up, when waiting my chance, I jammed my sword into his belly, which made him set up a prolonged, sharp cry. By constant vigilance and keeping from sleeping I contrived to fight the monsters off till daylight.[8]

Lieutenant Inman was rescued from the horrors of the Wheatfield on July 4. His wounds were severe enough to release him from further military service and he was eventually discharged in March 1864.[9]

In another episode concerning the hogs at Gettysburg, Private Charles Drake of Company C, 12th New Hampshire Volunteers, had a gruesome observation. Drake had his right leg amputated after it had been shattered by grapeshot during the second day's fighting. After the surgery the leg was simply thrown on a pile. Years after the war during a visit with Captain Richard Musgrove, also of the 12th New Hampshire, Drake was questioned about what became of his amputated leg. Drake's reply was, "The hogs ate it up." He further explained to Musgrove that he felt pain when the flesh was being torn from the bone as the pigs devoured it.[10]

So, on the battlefield of Gettysburg the tables were slightly turned and the hogs played the role of hunter at least for a time. But how horrible the time had to have been for those that became the hunted.

By the Crow of a Rooster

Many times in history the smallest piece of luck or detail can bring about the largest turn of events. The wounding or killing of a general has decided the outcome of many battles. A small mistake on a recipe and a new chemical is developed that can change the course of industry. History is loaded with examples, and the Civil War is no exception. One interesting story occurred on the high seas when a little bit of luck and attention to detail proved to be the turning point of the day.

The fog was thick as the USS *Montgomery* patrolled the Louisiana coastline. Lieutenant James E. Jouett strode on deck with his officer of the mid-watch. Suddenly, the distinct sound of a rooster could be heard in the mist. The lieutenant looked at his fellow officers and inquired if any chickens were brought on board when the ship last received supplies. No was the answer. Quickly Lieutenant Jouett ordered the crew to make ready to sail with a full head of steam. A blockade runner was on the move heading most certainly south to Havana, Cuba.[11]

During the Civil War blockade running was a game of cat and mouse. The Federal government had set up a blockade of the Southern coast. The purpose was to prohibit Southern traders from shipping cotton overseas and, more importantly, prevent much-needed supplies from entering the South.

Blockade runners, as they were called, were designed to be invisible on the ocean. The decks of these ships were generally close to the water line and painted a dull gray to be camouflaged and blend in with the horizon. Anthracite coal was the preferred fuel since hard coal generates little smoke compared to soft coal. However, hard coal was difficult to find as it is generally mined in the North. When exiting or entering a port, no lights or sounds were permitted on the runner. Everything involved with blockade running was designed to allow the runner to sneak past the Union patrols.[12]

The USS *Montgomery* was soon cutting through the water after its prey. At half past seven the fog finally lifted. Sailing just in front of the *Montgomery* was a schooner all sails set and flying the Louisiana state flag. Lieutenant Jouett was correct, the rebel boat was heading for Cuba, a popular destination of blockade runners. However, it wasn't long until the USS *Montgomery* gained the advantage in speed and shortly pulled alongside the Southern ship. Federal marines stood at the ready for the order to open fire. But bloodshed was not necessary as the rebel ship quickly surrendered.

Once on board, the captain of the runner inquired as to how Lieutenant Jouett detected his ship in such thick fog. "You have a rooster on board, and I heard him crow at four o'clock this morning," replied the lieutenant.

"I'll ring his neck," growled the captain of the runner.

To this Lieutenant Jouett snapped, "No, you won't. He's mine by right of capture."[13]

Luck was certainly on the side of Lieutenant Jouett that day. By paying attention to the small noise of a rooster crowing did he have the opportunity to catch his

Lieutenant James Jouett identified a blockade runner by the sound of a rooster.

Battles and Leaders of the Civil War

prize. Had the rooster been simply placed below the deck or kept quiet in some other way, Captain Jouett would never have known of the blockade runner cruise.

Rats, Rats, and More Rats

Civil War prisons were noted for their harsh conditions. Prisons in the North and South many times lacked adequate supplies to accommodate their boarders. Prisoners were often in need of clothing, shelter from the elements, and medical care. Another big item these men lacked was adequate food. Lieutenant Randolph Abbott Shotwell of the 8th North Carolina recalled that the soup served at the Fort Delaware prison near Philadelphia "was filled with white worms a half inch long," and that it was "to weak to drown the rice worms and pea bugs, which, however, came to their death by starvation."

Prisoners, out of necessity, became very resourceful in their procurement of food. One way to find relief from hunger was to feed on the rat population that was so prevalent in Civil War prisons. One prisoner who spent time at Johnson's Island on Lake Erie stated, "We traped for Rats and the Prisoners Eat Every one they Could get. I taken a mess of Fried Rats. They was all right to a hungry man, was liked Fried squirrels . . ." Joseph Ripley of Tennessee became so accomplished at rat catching he often gave banquets, stating that these feasts "broke the monotony of prison life, and to play host to a rat dinner . . . gave you the consciousness of having done well."[14]

Lieutenant Shotwell was not able to partake of the rat feasts at Fort Delaware, citing that his "mis-education" for rat meat somewhat spoiled his appetite for the creature. He did however record the habits of other prisoners in their quest for rodent nutrition.

The catching and eating of the huge rats which infest the island has become a common thing. It is a curious sight; grown men, whiskered and uniformed officers who have already "set a squadron in the field," lurking, club in hand, near one of the many breathing holes, which the long tailed rodents have cut in the hard earth, patiently awaiting a chance to strike a blow for "fresh meat and rat soup"—for dinner! They generally succeed in getting one or more rats at a sitting. Indeed the surface of the earth in some portions of the yard seems to be honeycombed by these amphibious burrowers, which are not the ordinary house rat, but the larger species of water rat, something like the Norway variety. They are eaten by fully a score of the officers, and apparently with relish. When deviled or stewed, they resemble young squirrels in the looks. I have not yet mustered stomach enough to nibble at one—though once—three years ago on the Potomac island—their brethren nibbled at me in no pleasant fashion. The flesh of these rodents is quite white, and when several are on a plate with plenty of dressing, they look so appetizing one cannot help regretting his early mis-education, or prejudice. That our antipathy to rats is all prejudice the rat eaters firmly assert. "Why," quoth one of them— "you eat wagon loads of hogs, and everybody knows a rat is cleaner than a hog. Rats are just as dainty as squirrels or chickens. . . .[15]

Rats also played an important part in the economy of prisons. Marcus B. Toney relates in his recollections *The Privations of a Private* that there was little currency being used at the Elmira Prison in southern New York state. Instead tobacco, pickles, pork bread, and rats were used in the exchange of goods. "Five chews of tobacco would buy a rat, a rat would buy five chews of tobacco, a loaf of bread would buy a rat, a rat would buy a loaf of bread, and so on. . . ."[16]

Many times rat catching was more like sport than a necessary function for survival. Captain W. A. Wash was a guest of the Federal government for several months at Johnson's Island on Lake Erie. In his book *Camp, Field and Prison Life* he relates a story of what occurred when three rats wandered into his room one night.

> That night three large rats came into the room, and one of the boys, being awake, closed the door on them. As it was hot we had left the door open and the top sash of the window out. Their scampering and lunging to escape soon waked the whole room, and two of the fellows, being somewhat nervous and tired, wanted to let the rats out. But as the majority ruled in our room, and we wanted to have some fun, the animals had to stay. It was a jollification from 3'clock till daylight, the rats racing over the floor, table, stove, shelves and beds, and frequently find the end of a leap right in our faces. One huge fellow crawled on my bunk near my head, and made a clear leap through a second story window. At daylight, after chasing the other two for awhile, we captured and beheaded them. So much for the rat story.
>
> Notwithstanding the following was the Lord's day, our prison witnessed a "ratastrophe" on a far more magnificent scale than the one just named. I was an eye witness and noted down at the time, "Sunday, 2 o'clock

P. M.—About forty rebels, with a little dog, ratting—
catch forty—some of the fellows going to make chicken
pie, and others squirrel fry of them—lots of rats and
fun." To give some idea of the respectability and rank
of our "rat club," I will just mention that Colonel John
A Fite, 7th Tennessee regiment, was its President, and
Lieutenant Billy Foote, son of Governor Foote, of Nashville, his chief-of-staff.[17]

Hospital Rats

One place noted to be free of vermin is hospitals—or
you would expect. During the Civil War, hospitals suffered from overcrowding, understaffing and lack of supplies and at some hospitals an overabundance of rats.
Unlike prisons, where rats were seen as a delicacy, in hospitals, they were a pestilence and the staff was charged with
getting rid of the pests. At Chimborazo Hospital in Richmond, Phoebe Yates Pember had a unique method for
catching the elusive rodents.

She intensely disliked the rats that inhabited the wards
stating they "ate all the poultices applied during the night to
the sick, and dragged away the pads stuffed with bran from
under the arms and legs of the wounded."

Preventing the rat thieves from doing harm was a chore
in itself as they were extremely hard to catch or kill. She wrote,
"They [rats] examined traps with the air of connoisseurs,
sometimes springing them from a safe position . . ."

However, Phoebe Pember was not going to be out-
smarted. She recalled, "I never had but one personal interview with any of them. An ancient gray gentleman, who
looked a hundred years old, both in years and depravity, would

eat nothing but butter, when that article was twenty dollars a pound; so finding all means of getting rid of him fail through his superior intelligence, I caught him with a fish-hook, well baited with a lump of his favorite butter, dropped into his domicile under the kitchen floor."[18]

Phoebe Pember doesn't relate what she did with the rat. But, it is probably safe to say that she didn't make stew of her catch.

Bad Water

In late June 1863 the Union Army of the Potomac was marching north in pursuit of the Confederate Army of Northern Virginia. This march would eventually end when the two armies met near the town of Gettysburg, Pennsylvania, on July 1–3. The three days at Gettysburg would be memorable for the men of the 116th Pennsylvania Volunteers. However, the march north would also be memorable for one particular incident.

The march north was fatiguing to the men. The days were hot. Dust filled the air from feet tramping the dirt roads. At the end of the second day of the pursuit the 116th reached Wolf Run Shoals on the Occoquan River in Virginia. As a member of the famed Irish Brigade the 116th was accustomed to the hardship of a soldier's life, having seen some of the worst fighting of the war at Fredericksburg and Chancellorsville. However, the sight of water was a blessing to these battle-hardened men and the idea of a cool bath enticing. Quickly camp was made for the evening and the men prepared themselves for a well-deserved dip in the cool, refreshing water. Without hesitation the soldiers shed their clothing and proceeded to skinny-dip.

The water was well worth the wait. Dirt from the day's march was soon a memory and the men were revived by the refreshing liquid. However, as they splashed, they noticed odd movements in the water as if something was wiggling past them on the river's surface. It was then that the men realized they were swimming with "enormous quantities of water snakes that infested the vicinity." Quickly the desire to bathe evaporated and a rout ensued unlike any that had ever been caused by the rebels.

Later that night after dark several officers decided it was their turn to partake of the welcoming waters of the Occoquan River. The men piled their clothes on the shore and entered the water. It wasn't long until they too received the chilling realization that they were bathing with snakes. "A match was lit and a sight met the bathers' eyes that horrified and amazed them. The whole strand was a mass of writhing, squirming serpents! Snakes of all sizes, short and long, thick and lean, in groups and tied in knots. Snakes single and by the dozen. Snakes by the hundred, countless and innumerable. What a scramble for clothes before the match went out! What an embarrassing predicament when it did! Dark as pitch, and a fellow's garments all tangled up with knots and rolls of serpents."[19]

Oddly enough a few snakes were able to accomplish what the Confederate army had been trying to do for over a year; that is, rout the Irish Brigade.

Pork for Dinner

Foraging was quite common for both armies during the Civil War. The idea of fresh chicken or pork was certainly inviting to men whose daily fare was salt pork and hardtack. However, foraging was dangerous. Farmers are usually not thrilled when their livestock is killed or stolen. In addition, contact with the opposing army was always a possibility. Because of these reasons numerous men put their lives in jeopardy for the taste of a fresh piece of ham or chicken.

Such was the experience of Private William H. Lee of Company D, 8th Iowa Cavalry. While serving on picket duty during the Atlanta Campaign, Private Lee learned that several hogs had been spotted between the Union and Confederate lines. With pistol in hand he slipped out between the lines in search of fresh pork. Private Lee traveled about a hundred yards when he spotted one of the hogs. In order to position himself for a shot, he had to straddle a stump that was about knee-high. However, before he could fire, a shot rang out and a ball hit the stump. Startled at this turn of events Private Lee explained, "I very suddenly made a right turn, but went only a few steps when a fine porker came running across my path. I shot at it while running and knocked it down, and I know that hog squealed louder and longer than any hog ever did before or since: but I ran up to it and shot it again, this time in the head, killing it instantly."

With supper now awaiting him, all Private Lee had to do was find a way to get the hog back to the safety of the Union lines. Ironically his problem was quickly solved, but with a unique twist. Private Lee explains further, "Just then I heard some one say: do you want all that hog? I looked up, and there not ten steps away and coming right up to me was a Johnnie soldier fully armed. I told him No, and he said, Can I have part? I answered, Certainly. He laid down his gun and accouterments, and with our pocket knives we soon divided that hog, he taking part and going one way and I the

Soldiers commonly used foraging to fill their haversacks.

Battles and Leaders of the Civil War

other part and going the other way. There were no questions asked and the war was not mentioned."[20]

Howling for His Master

For months and years after the Battle of Gettysburg relatives searched the battlefield for departed loved ones. This search was made easier for Northern families because the Federal dead had been collected and interred in the National Cemetery. However, immediately after the battle, Confederate dead were still considered to be enemy invaders and not given the same consideration as Union dead. Many Southerners were simply buried where they fell. It would be months and many times years before any of these men would be taken back to their homes for burial. One of the first Confederate dead to be recovered was Brigadier General William Barksdale.

Born in Tennessee, Barksdale moved to Mississippi where he was elected to Congress. At the outbreak of the war Congressman Barksdale took up the Southern cause and joined the Confederate army. He distinguished himself on most of the battlefields of the Eastern Theater. At Fredericksburg it was Barksdale's Mississippians who delayed the crossing of the Federals into the town. Using cellars and fences along the Rappahannock River, the men from Mississippi harassed Union engineers who were constructing pontoon bridges over the river.

Barksdale's Civil War career would come to an abrupt end during the second day at Gettysburg. Late in the afternoon Barksdale's Mississippians were ordered to strike the Union position held by Major General Daniel Sickles' III Corps located at the Peach Orchard. Barksdale, who had been anxious to make the assault, called to his men, "Attention, Mississippians! Battalions, Forward." Then "Fourteen hundred rifles were grasped with firm hands, and as the line officers repeated the command 'Forward March' the men sprang forward and fourteen hundred voices raised the famous 'Rebel yell'. . . ."[21] Barksdale was in the front leading the attack, his uniform looking every bit the soldier. "His short roundabout was trimmed on the sleeves with gold braid. The Mississippi button with a star in the center, closed it. The collar had three stars on each side next to the chin. Next his body was a fine linen or cotton shirt which was closed by three studs bearing Masonic emblems. His pants had two stripes of gold braid, half an inch broad, down each leg."[22]

The attack pushed the Union battle line back past the Peach Orchard toward the Trostle farm buildings. In doing so Barksdale's Mississippi Brigade was able to capture four guns from John Bigelow's 9th Massachusetts Battery. However, sometime during the assault Barksdale was hit and found later by Union troops west of Plum Run.[23]

The wounded general was taken to the house of Jacob Hummelbough (Hummelbaugh) located along the Taneytown Road.[24] Here a bed of blankets was made for him in the yard. Barksdale's wounds were examined by Assistant Surgeon Lieutenant Alfred T. Hamilton of the 148th Pennsylvania Volunteers.[25] Hamilton noted that Barksdale was "shot through the left breast from behind, and the left leg was broken by two missiles." The two men spoke for a short time and Barksdale asked if his wound was fatal. Hamilton could only answer that it was. Then sometime during the night William Barksdale breathed his last.[26]

Barksdale's body was buried in a temporary grave near the Hummelbaugh house. Like so many sons of the South who lost their lives so far away from home there was no ceremony. Only back home in his beloved South did mourners cry for the death of William Barksdale. The weeks and months passed into autumn until the first frost fell upon Adams County, Pennsylvania. It was then that Mrs. Barksdale was able to travel north to retrieve her husband's body. With her she brought a trusted companion, her husband's big black hunting dog.[27] Mrs. Barksdale was able to locate Dr. John W. C. O'Neal, a Gettysburg physician. Virginia-born Dr. O'Neal had kept a record of the Confederate dead on his travels throughout the area. It was this record that became the only directory of its kind.[28] With the help of Dr. O'Neil the new widow was able to locate her husband's grave near the Hummelbaugh farm.

It was during the exhumation of the body that a very strange incident occurred. As the soil was being removed from the general's grave, the dog began to bark and howl. The howling eventually grew into a wail as Barksdale's body was revealed. Once the body was recovered, the dog continued his sad wailing. As Mrs. Barksdale prepared to return home, she tried to

General William Barksdale's dog stayed by his grave even after his master's body had been removed.

MOLLUS-MASS Coll. at USAMHI

persuade the dog to come along, but her pleads were useless. The dog refused to leave the now empty grave site. Having no other recourse Mrs. Barksdale was forced to leave with her husband's body. Days passed and the dog still remained at his master's grave. Faithfully he protected the sacred ground, not allowing anyone to approach, and keeping visitors away with an angry snarl.[29] Finally, after days without food and water, the dog was found dead still guarding the grave of his beloved master.

Lice Racing

Graybacks, Tennessee Travelers, or, as they are more commonly called, lice were the scourge of both armies during the Civil War. Nobody was immune to infestation. From the lowest private to the highest generals they were all victims. John Billings wrote in his recollections, *Hardtack and Coffee*, that "Every soldier seemed foreordained to encounter this pest at close quarters."[30]

Today when people hear the word *lice* mentioned they feel an itch in their hair. Just the mere suggestion of this creature can have such an effect. Oddly lice are only attracted to clean hair. Therefore the idea that having lice suggests a person does not bathe is a fallacy. Another falsehood is the idea that lice jump or fly. The fact is they are a crawling creature and need to come in contact with an animal or person before they can climb aboard.

Having lice, as annoying and uncomfortable as it sounds, did have one small benefit. That was recreation. Civil War soldiers loved to gamble. So why not bet on something that was certainly in abundant supply? One way of using the louse for gambling was louse fighting. "A canteen side, having a circle marked off with charcoal, made a convenient arena. Contestants placed in the circle would, soldiers claimed, go at each other savagely, until one—and sometimes both—was hors de combat."[31]

Another form of louse gambling was the louse race. Sam Watkins of the 1st Tennessee Volunteers explained in his book *Co. Aytch* that "The lice were placed in plates—this was the race course—and the first that crawled off was the winner." However, a soldier had to be careful of what kind of louse they were dealing with, a four-legged kind or two-legged. Watkins noted that "If some fellow happened to catch a fierce-looking louse, he would call on Dornin for a race. Dornin would come and always win the stake." You would think it to be rather peculiar or extremely lucky that one man could have such a superior louse that wins every race. Well, it seems that Dornin's louse wasn't all that superior. Instead his louse was simply in a hurry to get off the plate Dornin always heated.[32]

Maybe the real louse was Dornin himself. Certainly when his companions found the secret to his success he was placed on the hot plate or at least the hot seat.

Animal Graffiti

When thinking of animals in the Civil War, horses and dogs usually come to mind, not turtles. These slow-moving creatures are hardly ever mentioned in Civil War literature with the exception of referring to soup or some slow-moving generals. Turtles are not soft and fuzzy nor do they wag their tails and lick their master's hand. However, the one thing that can be done with them is their shells can be carved. People will scratch their initials and a date into the shell of the turtle before allowing it to go free. That is just what one Ohio soldier did while campaigning in Tennessee. On the underside of a turtle the man carved "Union: Co. K, 26th Regt., Ohio Vols.; November 18, 1864."

The turtle was then either released or possibly gained its freedom by some other means. But when the war ended, the turtle was forgotten. For twenty years it lived in the vicinity of Chattanooga, Tennessee, until one day in 1884 it was picked up by a gentleman from the city. The gentleman, no doubt, was intrigued by the markings on the underside of the reptile and kept the turtle as a pet.

Two years later a group of veterans who had served in the 26th Ohio visited the Chattanooga area. The war years had faded and they were now simply on a tour of the South. It is supposed that some very strong memories of battles, death, and destruction were revisited on those days, a time in their youth that was better left alone. However, on this trip they also had the pleasure to revisit an old friend. Somehow the gentleman who was in possession of the turtle heard of the visit by the former soldiers and proceeded to show them his find. The Ohio men were delighted when, upon turning over the animal, they discovered their old unit's carving on its belly. One of the old veterans exclaimed, "He was a pet of some of our boys."[33]

Chapter Two

Predictions

A Substitute for Death

Private William Shuler enlisted in the 118th Pennsylvania Volunteers as a substitute.[1] This meant he was paid to replace a drafted man. Considered to be intelligent, Private Shuler claimed to be a lawyer and also a veteran of the Western Theater. Soon after joining Company I Shuler revealed his feelings that he would be killed in the next battle. The men of the company laughed at his prediction. To this Shuler replied, "Yes, you may laugh, but nevertheless it is true; for I see it just as plainly as if pictured on paper. But I do not care, for I shall go to my death just as I would go to a ball."[2]

The time had come for the spring campaign of 1864 to begin. The Army of the Potomac would, once again, attempt to advance upon Richmond. However, this time it would travel through a tangled mass of woodland called the Wilderness. The order to march arrived at the camp of the 118th on April 30.[3] When Shuler heard the news of the army's advance he advised his comrades that he had five more days to live.[4]

On May 3 instructions were finally given and the 118th left their winter quarters and proceeded south. By the next day they reached Germanna Ford on the Rapidan River and crossed on a pontoon bridge. Once across the river the men were given a break to rest. After three hours the regiment continued on its journey into the Wilderness until about 3 p.m. when it reached the Wilderness Tavern and bivouacked for the night.[5]

The next morning the men of the 118th busied themselves by constructing breastworks in preparation of a Confederate attack. The expected assault did not come and orders were issued for the troops to advance. Battle lines were formed with the 118th positioned in the second line adjacent to the 20th Maine.[6] The two lines of battle moved forward through the tangle of brush and trees. It wasn't long until the battle lines came to a clearing locally known as Saunders Field.[7] Here for the first time in the campaign the 118th experienced hostile fire. Major Holman S. Melcher of the 20th Maine recalled that "This field was less than a quarter of a mile across, had been planted with corn the year before, and was now dry and dusty. We could see the spurts of dust started up all over the field by the bullets of the enemy, as they spattered on it like big drops of a coming shower you have so often seen along a dusty road, but that was not the thing that troubled us. It was the dropping of our comrades from the charging line as they rushed across the fatal field with breasts bared to the terrible storm of leaden hail, and we knew that it would soon be our turn to run this fire."[8]

For Shuler the agony of watching his comrades fall had even more significance as he remembered his premonition. He turned to Sergeant Alfred Layman, "You see those works; well, just the other side of them I will fall; that is the spot. I know it! I know it!" The sergeant replied, "Do you honestly feel that such is your fate? If so, fall out, and do not go into the fight; I shall never mention it."

Private Shuler replied, "Sergeant I thank you; don't tempt: I have always done my duty, and shall do it now."[9]

Along the battle line the men moved forward across the field. Melcher recalled, "Pulling our hats low down over our eyes, we rushed across the field, and overtaking those of our comrades who had survived the fearful crossing of the front line, just as they were breaking over the enemy's lines, we joined with them in this deadly encounter, and there in that thicket of bushes and briers, with groans of the dying, the shrieks of the wounded, the terrible roar of the musketry and the shouts of command and cheers of encouragement, we swept them away before us like a whirlwind . . ."[10]

About fifty yards inside the Confederate works Private Shuler's premonition came true. With a thud a minié ball hit him in the left breast. Falling backwards Private Shuler landed in the arms of Sergeant Layman, who eased him to the ground. After placing his knapsack under his head, Layman asked if there was anything he could do. Private Shuler replied, "Yes, give me a drink of water." However, before he could sip a final drink, blood began to gush from the dying man's mouth. Sergeant Layman called for help to carry his friend from the field but Shuler refused, stating, "Sergeant, leave me where I am; it is no use; it is all up with me. Go on and take care of yourself."[11]

As the battle progressed, the advance of the Union line faltered, and the battle line was broken by the tangle of the brush. In addition rebel troops were discovered trying to out-flank the Union line. The 118th was ordered to retreat to the breastworks constructed earlier in the day.[12] Unfortunately the body of Private Shuler was left where he fell that May afternoon in the Wilderness and was never recovered.[13]

I Am Going To Fall

It is no wonder that soldiers had premonitions of death. Civil War casualty rates were high, especially as the war dragged on and soldiers became better at killing each other. Seeing ones friends and comrades being wantonly killed certainly had to give men the idea that they too were vulnerable to death. One man who felt that death was very near was First Sergeant Thomas Innis Woods of Company B, 155th Pennsylvania Volunteers. He was called "one of the bravest and most energetic men in the Company, who had been promoted from the ranks." But a strange feeling of dread overtook him. So strong was that feeling that he approached his commanding officer, Captain Henry W. Grubbs, and asked to be relieved from the next day's combat. Captain Grubbs asked if Sergeant Woods was sick or injured in some way, to which Woods could only admit the negative. The captain refused the request, stating that every man was needed in the ranks, and if Sergeant Woods was relieved of duty, why not the next guy?

The regiment had just passed through the nightmare of the Battle of the Wilderness in which the two great armies battled to a standstill in a tangle of brush and trees. Now the Union Army of the Potomac needed a new strategy in its quest to capture the Confederate capital of Richmond. The plan was simply to outflank the Confederate Army of Northern Virginia with the objective to secure Spotsylvania Court House.

The V Corps would lead the flanking movement. The Union column set out at eight thirty on the evening of May 7, 1864. The 155th had the honor of spearheading the flanking movement followed by the rest of the Union V Corps. The column made slow time as they advanced on the Brock Road toward Spotsylvania. The night was dark and the road narrow, causing much consternation for the men of the 155th. In addition Confederate cavalry barricaded the way by felling trees across the road.[14]

During one point of the march the men were given several minutes to rest. At this time it was observed that "Sergeant Woods was seen to leave the ranks and seat himself at the foot of a large tree, where he took from his pocket a diary and made entries therein."[15] Soon the men were ordered back into the column and continued their trek. Finally, at about eight thirty the next morning the column emerged from the woods onto the Alsop Farm only two and a half miles from their goal of Spotsylvania Court House. In front of their position, across the fields, lay Laurel Hill, where Confederate troops could be seen throwing up a quick breastwork of fence rails. Unfortunately, Confederate General Robert E. Lee surmised that the best strategy for the Union army was to move to Spotsylvania Court House. Taking advantage of his position of interior lines, Lee was able to march the shorter distance and dig in on Laurel Hill.

Major General Gouverneur Warren, commander of the V Corps, surmised that there was no time to lose in attacking the rebel position before they had a chance to throw up proper entrenchments. This was unwelcomed news to the men. The day was already becoming unseasonably hot. In addition the men were exhausted from their nightlong march and having had no breakfast that morning.[16]

The order was issued to drive the rebels from their position. Before assaulting Laurel Hill the Union column had to advance through a piece of woods. Approaching within two to three hundred yards the column was hit by severe musketry fire from the tree line. It was quickly surmised that the rebels were stationed behind a breastwork of logs and rails.[17] Before any further attempt was made on Laurel Hill the woods had to be secured. As the first Union regiments, making the assault, gave way to the rebel fire, another line moved forward, which included the 155th. With a brass band urging them on, the Union line charged the breastworks. Again the Confederate fire was too much.[18] To make matters worse, another rebel force had flanked the attack and positioned themselves in a wood to the right of the Union line. With fire now coming from the front and side the attack had to be called off until later in the day when more troops could be called forward.[19]

During roll call after the battle Sergeant Woods was reported as missing. Sergeant James McMillian and several other men began to search for their missing comrade and found his body in a wooded area. Upon examining the corpse the men found his diary. The last entry was addressed to Sergeant McMillian. In it Sergeant Woods reaffirmed the belief he would be killed, stating, "I am going to fall to-day. If you find my body, I desire you to bury it and mark my grave so that if my friends desire to take it home they can find it. Please read the Ninetieth Psalm at my burial."[20] The entry also gave instructions as to the disposition to be made of his watch and personal effects.[21]

Thomas Innis Woods, shown here in the Zouave uniform of the 155th Pennsylvania Volunteers, predicted his own death at Spotsylvania.

Under the Maltese Cross

A Campaign Too Long

During the Civil War many men, facing the prospect of death, found themselves very much interested in religion. Both Confederate and Union armies experienced periods of revival when men turned to the Bible and God for answers and comfort. This was especially true "when large-scale fighting was in prospect."[22] The knowledge that high casualty rates were soon going to be filling the halls of heaven and hell would certainly convince even the firmest nonbeliever to acquire some type of faith.

One of these men was Sergeant Fred Sheckler of Company K, 155th Pennsylvania Volunteers. Upon enlisting in September 1862 Sergeant Sheckler did not think much about religion. The men of the 155th found themselves in many of the hotly contested battles fought by the Army of the Potomac. As a witness to this horror, thoughts of the afterlife must have weighed heavily on his mind. By May 1864 Sergeant Sheckler apparently had a change of heart. Sergeant D. Porter Marshall recalled he "now became interested and we trust was truly converted and surrendered himself wholly to the keeping of his Saviour."

Soon after his conversion Sheckler expressed to his brother-in-law, Private William Whited, and Sergeant Marshall that he did not expect to live through the next campaign. The two men tried to persuade their depressed comrade that he was being foolish, but to no avail. Instead Sergeant Sheckler asked that they take care of his watch and several other personal items. He especially wanted them to write his wife and children to inform them of his fate.[23]

Jericho Ford where the 155th Pennsylvania crossed the North Anna River in pursuit of the Confederate Army of Northern Virginia.

MOLLUS-MASS Coll. at USAMHI

On May 23, 1864, the men of the 155th were in pursuit of General Robert E. Lee's Confederate Army of Northern Virginia, which was retreating toward Richmond. While in pursuit the 155th approached the North Anna River at a crossing known as Jericho Ford. At the ford the swift-running river was three to four feet deep. However, there was no time to be lost waiting for the construction of pontoon bridges. It was already three o'clock in the afternoon and the crossing had to be made before nightfall.[24] Immediately the men of the 155th were ordered into the water. Haversacks and rifles were held high to keep them dry as the column struggled to the opposite shore. Many men had difficulty fighting the current in the deep water. For the six-foot-tall Sheckler the crossing wasn't a problem.

Once on the southern shore, a battle line was immediately formed that advanced to an edge of a timberline. The men of the 155th waited patiently, guarding against any surprise attack while the remainder of the brigade crossed the river. The men were allowed to relax when the entire brigade was safely across. They stacked their guns and prepared for supper.[25]

By this time Sheckler should have felt that his premonition was wrong. The Wilderness Campaign was well under way being in its eighteenth day. However, fate was not to be denied. At about six o'clock, before the men could partake of their meal, the rebel yell echoed through the woods in front of the Union position. Immediately out of the trees ran a conglomeration of cattle, hogs, sheep, and turkeys struggling to flee the advancing rebels. All along the Union line troopers rushed to their weapons that had been stacked. The men of the 155th dropped to their knees and waited for the rebel onslaught.[26] Troopers clearing brush in the front rushed back to the main line. With the Southern line still in the woods, the Pennsylvanians could not see their foe but knew they were close as the distinctive rebel yell could clearly be heard, prompting the men to fire at the noise. Major John Ewing of Company H shouted, "Boys, as long as you keep up such a fire as that was, no troops in the world can charge up to you."[27] The Confederate attack was repulsed. But the fight wasn't over. Three more times the Southern battle line assaulted the Union position and three more times it was thrown back, with the last one occurring after dark.[28]

For Sergeant Sheckler the campaign had gone too long and his premonition had come true. During one of the

Confederate assaults he received a fatal bullet wound to the head and died instantly.[29]

Death Times Three

There is a superstition that things come in threes. Marriages, deaths, and babies are just examples. Many times this superstition seems to come true. For the men of Company F, 16th New York Volunteers, it certainly was a reality. On May 6, 1862, the 16th New York was engaged in the Peninsula Campaign. Their objective on this day was to secure the area of West Point, Virginia, at the head of the York River. This was an attempt to cut off the Confederate army that was retreating toward Richmond. The men of the 16th and remainder of the division under the command of General William Franklin were put ashore at Eltham's Landing on the Eltham plantation.[30] After landing, the men stacked their arms and ate supper. Once finished with the evening meal they sat down to talk away the remaining hours of the day before getting some sleep.

During the conversation Private Edwin Bishop delivered some somber news. He said, "Boys, if I should fall in the next battle, as I now believe I shall, I wish you would bury me under this tree, where I indicate by these lines." The normally lighthearted and fun-provoking soldier marked off, with a spade, the outline of a grave.

As if the thought were contagious, Corporal George Love rose from his seated position and taking the spade, remarked, "I would like you to dig my grave beside Bishop's, but please dig it with more regularity than his crooked lines indicate; I am the son of a sexton and have helped to dig many." Then with the spade Corporal Love scratched out his design and sat back down.

Next in line was Private Peter Ploof. Picking up the spade, he proceeded to instruct his friends, saying, "If I fall, dig my grave here beside Love's, and do it as we dig graves at home. Please follow the lines I make for you." Quietly he drew out the lines of a coffin used at the time period where the box was wider at the shoulders and tapered toward the feet.

Early the next morning at 3 a.m. the men of Companies F and G were ordered to picket in a wood line that bordered the plantation. A Confederate attack was expected as rebel infantry and cavalry had been seen on the outskirts of the plantation since the Union force landed. At about nine o'clock a rebel column, the Texas Brigade commanded by General John Bell Hood, emerged from the woods in front of the pickets. The Confederate force was surprised that they had run into Federal troops so quickly. To prevent any friendly fire incidents in the heavy woods, orders had been given that men in the assaulting column not load their weapons. Rifles were quickly loaded and the command given to move forward. The two companies were unable to stall the Southern advance and had to give way to the overwhelming foe. The pickets ran back to the Union main line, which was able to put up a fight with their Southern counterparts. However, they too were eventually driven back toward the river. The Union command retreated for about a mile when Federal artillery on the river transports opened fire.

Seeing that their objective of keeping the Federal force on the river was accomplished, the rebel attack was called off. When the guns finally fell silent, Company F had only three fatalities: Bishop, Love, and Ploof. All three were granted their final wishes of being buried side by side under the tree they had selected the previous night.[31]

Death Had No Favorites

Death played no favorites during the Civil War. From the lowliest privates to highest ranking generals death was always present. The Battle of Gettysburg was no exception to this rule. During the three-day battle numerous high ranking officers were killed including Generals John Reynolds, William Barksdale, Lewis Armistead, William Garnett, and Samuel Zook.[32]

To these men the idea that death was a possibility was certain. Having been in numerous battles before, they certainly had to understand the consequences of entering upon such deadly work. Still each man was in the midst of the fighting when he was struck down.

Even though he had to understand the idea that death was always close by, Samuel Zook came to realize that his death was even closer. During the morning of July 2 Zook was paid a visit from Jacob Cole, who had a presentiment that he would either be wounded or killed during the day's fighting. Cole, a member of the 57th New York Volunteers, asked Zook to take charge of a large sum of money. Zook replied, "My boy, you must not have such feelings, but if you are afraid I will give you a pass to go into the Ambulance corps."

Cole, not wanting to be known as a coward, stated, "No, General, I have never deserted my comrades in battle and I do not intend to desert them now. If I am killed I shall be killed doing my duty." The general, hearing this reply, took the money from Cole for safekeeping. However, soon after,

General Zook summoned Cole back to his headquarters, "My boy, I have the same sensations you have—that I will be killed—and you had better take the money and give it to some one else."[33]

Brigadier General Samuel Zook was born in Chester County, Pennsylvania, but spent most of his childhood living at Valley Forge on the same ground that the American Army of the Revolution spent the winter of 1777–78.[34] Defying his Mennonite-Amish ancestry Zook became associated with a military life.[35] He served in both the Pennsylvania and New York militias. Soon after the Civil War began, Zook recruited the 57th New York and was commissioned its colonel. By December 1862 Zook was in command of a brigade. During the Union debacle of Fredericksburg he was wounded but was awarded the star of brigadier general for his performance while storming Marye's Heights.[36]

During the afternoon of July 2, 1863, Brigadier General Zook's brigade was positioned near the center of the Union line. Off to their left could be heard the fighting around the Devil's Den and Wheatfield. In this wheatfield, owned by a local farmer named George Rose, Union and Confederate forces would do battle for much of the afternoon. The twenty-six-acre field of wheat would change hands several times and go down in history as the Whirlpool of the battle.[37] Some historians have even gone as far as to say that this small area of land was the bloodiest spot in the Western Hemisphere.

As the fighting gained momentum and reinforcements were summoned, General Zook halted for a second near the Irish Brigade whose men were receiving absolution from Father William Corby. Today the story of this scene is told countless times. For General Zook it was no less thrilling. Turning to his aide, Colonel James D. Brady, Zook remarked, "My God! Brady, that was the most impressive sight I have ever heard of."[38]

Soon Zook's Third Brigade was ordered to the Wheatfield. The noise of battle grew louder as the brigade made its way through the Weikert Woods. Zook noticed the disorganized state of the Union troops on the field. Fearing that they would slow the progress of his brigade, he shouted, "If you can't get out of the way lie down, and I will march over you." The men were ordered to lie down and Zook's troops marched over them onto the field of battle.

Not long after entering the Wheatfield, a musket ball hit Zook in the abdomen. Turning to his aide, Colonel Josiah Favill, the wounded man said, "It's all up with me, Favill."[39] Before falling from his horse, Zook was caught by Colonel Favill and Captain Broom of his staff.[40]

The general was taken to the G. E. Hoke Tollhouse on the Baltimore Pike where he began his struggle against death. The next day, July 3, the battle resumed. When Confederate artillery fire hit close to the Hoke house, Zook was moved even farther to the rear. As the general's life slowly faded,

Brigadier General Samuel Zook was mortally wounded only moments after leading his brigade into the Wheatfield at Gettysburg.

MOLLUS-MASS Coll. at USAMHI

Colonel Favill offered to summon a minister, but Zook declined, stating that "it was too late." The general had resigned himself to his fate and waited for death to visit. As the day wore on, the noise of battle grew and the sounds of Pickett's Charge reached the ears of the wounded general.[41] Curious as to the reason for the noise Zook sent Colonel Favill to investigate. Upon his return Favill brought the good news that Pickett had been repulsed, reporting "that the bands had been ordered to the front, flags were flying, and the enemy were in retreat."[42]

Zook lingered between life and death for a little while longer. But, by 5 p.m. his battle was over, and death claimed another soul from the Wheatfield of Gettysburg.[43]

Black Is the Color of the Day

Colonel Edward Cross was a warrior who knew no fear in battle. He once said, "Having received nine wounds in the present war (Civil War) and three in other wars, I am not afraid of rebel bullets."[44] However, the thirty-one-year-old brigade commander did have a feeling that his life on earth was soon to be ended. On the morning of June 27 in a conversation about the upcoming battle he revealed his fear to Second Lieutenant Charles Hale, "It will be my last battle." In addition he stated, "Mr. Hale, I wish you to attend to my books and papers. That private box of mine in the headquarters wagon—you helped me to re-pack it the other day. After the campaign is over, get it at once, dry the contents if damp, and then turn it over to my brother Richard."

The days passed and the Army of the Potomac made its way north chasing the Confederate Army of Northern Virginia to the town of Gettysburg, Pennsylvania. During the march Lieutenant Hale was uncomfortable with the statements of his commander, resenting the fact that Colonel Cross would speak in such a way. But, once again the subject emerged when Cross confided in the young nineteen-year-old Lieutenant Hale, "Mr. Hale: attend to that box of mine at the first opportunity."

On July 2 the Battle of Gettysburg was raging at full strength. The II Corps to which Cross's brigade belonged, was posted near the center of the Union line. The men rested and waited to be called into action.[45] During this wait Colonel Cross approached some men of the brigade. After speaking to them for a while, he said, "Boys, you know what's before you. Give 'em hell!" To this the men responded, "We will, Colonel."[46]

In their front and left the battle soon opened as Confederate attacks struck the Union army's III Corps under Major General Daniel Sickles. With the action nearby growing desperate for the Union army, Colonel Cross prepared himself to meet his fate. Lieutenant Hale describes what transpired in those moments before orders finally came to move forward:

> The Colonel had for some time been walking back and forth in his quick, nervous way, his hands clasped behind his back, a habit that was usual with him. Presently, stopping short near where I was standing, he drew out from an inside pocket a large, new, black silk handkerchief. Arranging it in folds on his lifted knee, then handing me his hat to hold, he quickly swathed his head with it in turban fashion, tying the two ends behind. We had seen him do this on other fields with a

red bandana and it then amused me somewhat, but under the peculiar circumstances of the few days previous the black handkerchief was appalling. Again he took off his hat saying, "Please tie it tighter, Mr Hale." My hands were trembling as I picked at the knot. "Draw it tighter still," he said impatiently, and finally I adjusted it to suit him.

It was at this time that II Corps commander Major General Winfield Scott Hancock rode up to Cross. Hancock, still on his horse, looked at Cross and gravely remarked, "Colonel Cross, this day will bring you a star." Cross looked at his commanding general and shook his head. "No, General, this is my last battle." The two men then parted to attend to the business at hand.[47]

Soon after his encounter with Hancock, Colonel Cross approached Surgeon William Child of the 5th New Hampshire. To Surgeon Child, Cross gave a "massive gold ring, some valuable papers, a pocket book, and some other valuables." Cross then said, "Good-bye! It will be an awful day. Take care of yourself, I must go into the fight, but I fear I shall be killed. Good-bye."[48]

At about five o'clock orders were received to move forward. The brigade quickly moved toward the now famous Rose Wheatfield. The brigade formed into line of battle and pushed through the Weikert Woods onto the Millertown Road (modern Wheatfield Road). Bullets from rebel skirmishers soon filled the air. Colonel Cross and his staff dismounted to reduce their exposure to the enemy fire.

By now the battle was becoming very hot in the Wheatfield. Lieutenant Hale wrote years later:

As we emerged from the woods into the open ground, the bullets from the enemy's skirmishers came buzzing around like bees, and we could see puffs of smoke from their rifles in every direction, showing that we were about to encounter a heavy force. The line was moving up a slight rise of ground in front, and here we all dismounted, giving the horses in charge of the orderlies. Just as the heads of the men in the ranks cleared the crest of the rise, the enemy posted in the edge of the woods down back of the stone wall on the south side of the field at once opened on us, and halting just on the crest, our line opened fire in return. . . . The wheat had been trampled into the dirt by line after line before we came. Lying flat on the ground, firing at us over the crest as we advanced was a line of the enemy's skirmishers, but we moved so quickly that they could not get back, and jumping up from the ground they rushed back through our line.

"Get a file of men for a guard and hold them, Mr. Hale," shouted Colonel Cross.

Moments later Colonel Cross informed his aides, "Boys—instruct the commanders to be ready to charge when the order is given. Wait here for the command, or, if you hear the bugles of the Fifth New Hampshire on the left, move forward on the run." Cross then moved over near the 5th New Hampshire on the far left of the brigade line.[49] It was here that fate intervened. A rebel soldier mounted on top of a large boulder sighted the colonel and fired, hitting him in the abdomen. The ball passed through Cross' body and exited near the spine.[50]

Colonel Edward Cross wore a black handkerchief on his head the day he was mortally wounded.

Colonel Cross was immediately taken from the field. However, his fate was sealed. During the night Cross was comforted by his brother, Major Richard Cross, and the surgeons of the brigade.[51] Finally at about 12:30 a.m. on July 3 Colonel Cross spoke his last, "I did hope I would live to see peace, and our country restored. I have done my duty. I think the boys will miss me. O welcome death. All my effects I give to my mother. Say farewell to all." With those words Colonel Cross' premonition was fulfilled.[52]

Death in the Wheatfield

"It is with feelings of the most profound sorrow that I take this, the very first spare moment, to give you the sad intelligence of the death of your brother-in-law, Capt. Robert M. Forster . . ." News of this type traveled home all too often during the four years of the Civil War. This letter was written by Captain Robert H. Forster of Company A, 148th Pennsylvania Volunteers, on July 6, 1863, to notify the family that Captain Robert McKay Forster of Company C had met his fate in the Wheatfield at Gettysburg.[53] Captain Forster was a man who had a lot to lose. He was blessed with "a wife and three boys at home, was an intelligent, progressive farmer and merchant and occupied a leading position in his community." Like many volunteers he had strong convictions, leading him to join the service.[54] But Captain Forster knew something was wrong. It was a feeling that his wife was soon be to widowed and his three boys fatherless. In March 1863 he had a premonition of being killed in the first battle in which he was engaged. The feelings were so strong that he approached Colonel James Beaver, commander of the 148th. Beaver tried to make light of the premonition, but Forster was persistent. He asked Beaver to help him prepare a will. With his affairs in order, Forster went about his duties.[55]

In the spring of 1863 the 148th was a fairly new regiment in the Army of the Potomac, having only been mustered into service during September 1862.[56] The first opportunity for battle was at Chancellorsville in May. Only four companies of the 148th saw any action during this battle. Company C was one of these companies. However, Captain Forster was seriously ill and unable to serve. In a letter he wrote, "I have been very sick and am not much better yet. I can hardly hold my head up to write these few lines." Captain Forster was taken to a hospital in Washington and then permitted to return home to Centre County, Pennsylvania, to recuperate from his illness. By May 31 he was back with the army just in time for the Gettysburg Campaign.

In June the Confederate Army of Northern Virginia began its invasion of Pennsylvania. Once they realized that the Confederates were invading the North, the Union Army of the Potomac followed in pursuit. For the men of the 148th it was a grueling task. Captain Forster wrote to his wife, "We marched some days as much as twenty miles and for the first four days of our march I have never felt the heat so in my life. The dust in the road was many times shoe-mouth deep. The soldiers gave out by hundreds and it was nothing uncommon to see men drop down as if dead from sunstroke, and in some cases they never recovered."[57]

The 148th arrived on the Gettysburg Battlefield at 9 p.m. on July 1, 1863. The first day's fight was complete and the men were ordered to form into a line of battle and lay on their arms. That night Private Lemuel Osman remembered falling asleep while listening to Captain Forster praying that

God would be with him (Forster) and the rest of the regiment. The next day the 148th saw little action until late in the afternoon when the regiment was ordered to the Wheatfield to halt the Confederate attack on the left of the Union line.[58]

The men of the 148th moved by the double-quick to the threat on the left. Before reaching the Wheatfield a halt was called. The 148th formed into a line of battle with the remainder of the regiments in the brigade. On the far right stood the 61st New York. To their left the 81st Pennsylvania filed into line. Next, the 148th positioned themselves, and on the far left the 5th New Hampshire. The Union troops marched into the Wheatfield a short distance when another halt was called. After several minutes the brigade was ordered forward. In front rebel troops were positioned behind a stone fence. A volley was fired into the gray troopers and they began to break.[59] Captain Forster yelled to the men of Company C, "They are falling back, boys; forward!" Soon after, a minié ball plunged into Forster's head, killing him instantly. Private Osman remembered, "The barrel of my gun had got hot and dry and I couldn't force a ball down. I stepped back and told Captain Forster, who told me to throw it down and hunt another. I

Captain Robert Forster predicted he would be killed at Gettysburg.

The Story of Our Regiment: A History of the 148th Pennsylvania Volunteers

threw it down, ran along the line, got one in Company I. When I came back the Captain was dead; the blood was running down his cheek. I picked up his cap and laid it on his head, but did not think of getting what was in his pockets."[60] Sergeant John Benner, a colorbearer, picked up Captain Forster's sword and belt for safekeeping. The next winter he was able to return home and presented the articles to Forster's sister.

Unfortunately, any other valuables the captain had on his person were stolen by rebel looters who wandered onto the battlefield searching for such articles. Private Robert M. Wadding of Company I had been wounded and remained on the field that night. He recalled later that he lay close by the body of Captain Forster and watched as looters robbed the corpse of a pocketbook from the dead man's side pocket. Such was the sad experience of Captain Robert Forster.[61]

Chapter Three

Coincidences

A Meeting of the Irish

Private James Whitty was an Irishman in Company A, 6th Wisconsin Volunteers, part of the famed Iron Brigade. During the war Whitty was wounded four times, at Gainesville, South Mountain, Fitz Hugh's Crossing, and the Wilderness.[1] Of these four, two are notable. At South Mountain his wounding created some comic relief for the men of the regiment. After jumping up on a rock, Whitty began firing at the Confederate line. Suddenly he was hit. Jumping off the rock, he yelled, "For the love of God, a 'Wild Irishman' is hit."[2]

During the Battle of the Wilderness Whitty received his last wound, this one in the leg, which had to be amputated. Worse yet, he was a prisoner and the procedure was done by a Confederate surgeon.

After the surgery the rebel doctor spoke to Whitty. He was an Irishman and noticed that Whitty was also of Irish stock. The surgeon inquired of his patient's name. "James Whitty," was the reply. Quickly the surgeon became more interested and asked Whitty if his father's name was John, and was he born in Cork, Ireland? Whitty answered yes. The doctor was surprised and remarked, "My dear boy, your father and I were boys together and very warm friends, the best we have shall be yours." By mere coincidence James Whitty's luck turned about and he did receive the best treatment possible from his father's old friend.[3]

Whitty survived his captivity and the war. However, for years afterward he suffered from his South Mountain wound, the ball from which had never been removed. Eventually James Whitty succumbed to this wound and died from complications in 1906.[4]

A Knapsack's Return

Civil War battlefields were a treasure trove of discarded debris. Knapsacks, muskets, photographs, any item a soldier carried could be found waiting to be claimed. Generally to the victor of these battles went the spoils of war, and many times soldiers were more than happy to lay claim to some much-needed article. Often times Southern troops benefited most from these spoils of war since they were more than likely to be underequipped when compared to their Northern counterparts.

One Confederate soldier was quick to claim a Yankee knapsack on the First Bull Run Battlefield near the Henry House Hill. It was a fine knapsack and would do well for his needs. Its former owner was a member of the 21st Massachusetts Volunteers with the initials J. M. S., which were painted on the side of the sack.

The man carried the knapsack through several engagements until September 17, 1862. It was during the Battle of Antietam that the soldier fell prey to a Union minié ball while fighting near the Burnside Bridge. Coincidently the 21st

Massachusetts was also positioned in this area. Late in the day, after the battle had ceased, a member of the 21st began to search for fallen comrades close to the bridge. Coming to a stone wall the man noticed a dead rebel—which was not unusual. However, what caught his eye was the knapsack lying next to the body. On the side of the knapsack were the initials J. M. S. along with the words *21st Massachusetts*. Picking up the sack the man realized that it was the same knapsack he had painted for James Madison Stone.[5]

Met Bullets

What is the possibility of two minié balls meeting in mid-air? Even without doing some complicated mathematical calculations, one can say the chance is rare. However, every once in a while when reading Civil War literature the subject is broached momentarily.

Mrs. Roger Pryor in her book *Reminiscences of Peace and War* relates a story of an interview she had with General and Mrs. Ulysses S. Grant. The meeting took place in New York City twenty years after the war. During the conversation Mrs. Pryor brought forth a pair of met bullets. She exclaimed, "the bullets are welded together so as to form a perfect horseshoe— a charm to keep away witches and evil spirits."

Mrs. Roger Pryor displayed two bullets that had collided in midair to General and Mrs. Ulysses S. Grant.

Reminiscences of Peace and War

General Grant looked at the met bullets and replied, "Those are minie balls, shot from rifles of equal caliber. And they met precisely equidistant to a hair. This is very interesting, but it is not the only one in the world. I have seen one other, picked up at Vicksburg."

Mrs. Pryor went on to tell the general that the met bullets were found near Fort Gregg outside Petersburg, Virginia, at the end of the war. Even though they are not the only met bullets in a war in which millions of rounds were fired, they were certainly an object of much curiosity.[6]

A Message Delivered

There are many incidents of fraternizing between Union and Confederate pickets during the Civil War—friendly words between enemies who carefully watched each other while trying to be somewhat civil. Even exchanging coffee for tobacco was not uncommon. However, sometimes these conversations between pickets become somewhat interesting. The following incident was written by Mrs. R. H. Dudley and published in the *Confederate Veteran* Magazine in February 1892:

> Soon after the battle of Murfreesboro (or Stone's River) 1863, Mr. Charles Eckles, of the _____ Illinois Regiment (Company D, 34th Illinois Infantry), was sent as a guard to the home of my father, (Mr. Kit Beesley). He remained there several months and was then sent to Rosecran's Army at Chattanooga, just before the battle of Chickamauga. Mr Eckles told my mother, when he bade her good-bye, that if he should be fortunate enough to meet her boys on picket and

they would give him a letter he would send it to her. She had not heard from them in a long time.

Fate decreed they should meet. While on Federal picket duty he hailed the Confederate picket and asked what command he belonged to. His reply was "First Tennessee Infantry, Cheatham's Division." He then asked his name and was told, "Wm. Beesley." The Federal picket said, "I am just from your father's house and they have not heard from you in a long time. I told your mother if I was fortunate enough to meet her boys on picket duty and they would give me a letter, I would send it to her." My brother wrote the letter, gave it to him and my mother received it in due time. It was hailed with joy, of course.

That was the last we heard of Mr. Eckles until the opening of Chickamauga Park last September. He is a member of the G.A.R. and stopped over at Murfreesboro and went to see my mother and brother whom he had met on the picket line in 1863. He was gladly received by all.[7]

Meeting at the Hornet's Nest

In today's world, battles are viewed on television screens literally as they happen or recreations shown on the big screen in epic movies. However, people living in the nineteenth century did not have this modern technology. They relied on stereoptic cards that allowed photos to be seen in three dimensions. Another way of witnessing the great battles of the past was by viewing a cyclorama painting. A cyclorama is a huge painting on a 360 degree canvas that places the viewer in the center of the action. One of the most famous cycloramas depicts Pickett's Charge during the Battle of Gettysburg and can still be viewed today. Other Civil War battles such as the Battle of Atlanta and Shiloh were also painted and put on display for the public's benefit.

The exhibit of the Shiloh Cyclorama in Chicago was met with much interest. Young and old alike paid the 50 cent fee to see the carnage of the battle as painted on the 400-foot giant canvas.[8] Included among the sightseers were old veterans. Past their prime and often wielding canes, these men viewed the cyclorama with a different kind of interest. They analyzed the painting and reminisced about the part they played in the great battle.

One area of the painting called the "Hornet's Nest" was of particular interest to spectators. During the first day of the Battle of Shiloh the "Hornet's Nest" was a scene of horrific fighting. As the Union army retreated from the advancing Confederates, portions of several divisions were able to rally and form a defensive line. A piece of high ground was chosen where an old wagon road fronted a thick underbrush supplying cover. In addition, in front of the road was an open field over which Confederate assaults had to be made. During the afternoon several assaults were made on the half-mile Union line until it was finally broken.[9]

The *Chicago News* reported an incident that occurred during one of the showings of the cyclorama as two old veterans crossed paths while examining the action of the "Hornet's Nest."

One, a small shriveled up man with gray whiskers dressed in black. The other a tall, raw-boned man wearing gray and a military slouch hat. As the two men neared each other, the man in gray inquired,

". . . Reckon you were at Shiloh, eh, stranger?" asked the tall, rawboned man.

"Yes," replied the small shriveled-up man, "and I shall never forget it; it was the toughest battle of the war."

"I was thar," said the tall, raw boned man, "and my regiment was drawn up right over yonder where you see that clump of trees."

"You were a rebel then?"

"I was a Confederate," replied the tall, raw-boned man, "and I did some right smart fighting among that clump of trees that day."

"I remember it well," said the small, shriveled-up man, "for I was a Federal soldier, and the toughest scrimmage in all that battle was just among that clump of trees."

"Prentiss was the Yankee General," remarked the tall, raw-boned man. "and I'd have given a pretty to have seen him that day. But, doggone me, the little cuss kept out of sight, and we'uns came to the conclusion he was hidin' back in the rear somewhar."

"Our boys were after Marmaduke," said the small, shriveled-up man, "for he was the rebel General and had bothered us a great deal. But we could get no glimpse of him—he was too sharp to come to the front, and it was lucky for him, too."

"Oh; but what a scrimmage it was!" said the tall, raw-boned man.

"How the sabers clashed and how the Minies whistled!" cried the small, shriveled-up man.

The panorama brought back the old time with all the vividness of yesterday's occurrence. The two men were filled with a strange yet beautiful enthusiasm.

"Stranger," cried the tall, raw-boned man, "we fought each other like devils that day and we fought to kill. But the war's over now, and we ain't soldiers any longer—gimme your hand!"

"With pleasure," said the small, shriveled-up man, and the two clasped hands.

"What might be your name?" inquired the tall, raw boned man.

"I am General B. [Benjamin] M. Prentiss," said the small, shriveled-up man.

"The——you say!" exclaimed the tall raw-boned man.

"Yes," reaffirmed the small, shriveled-up man; "and who are you?"

"I," replied the tall, raw-boned man, "I am General John S. Marmaduke."[10]

Finally after twenty-three years two old adversaries of the "Hornet's Nest" came face to face. Like many of the old veterans of the Civil War the former anger had passed and bodies had grown old with the war now a distant memory.

Generals Benjamin M. Prentiss, *left*, and John S. Marmaduke, *right*, were adversaries who finally met years after their bloody struggle at the Hornet's Nest.

MOLLUS-MASS Coll. at USAMHI and *Battles and Leaders of the Civil War*

With A Leg Between Them

Henry J. and Levi J. Walker were brothers from Mecklenburg County, North Carolina. Nineteen-year-old Levi was a farmer while twenty-four-year-old Henry made his living as a school teacher. Both men heard the call to arms for the Southern cause and went to war together on May 20, 1861. The men enlisted as privates in Company B, 13th North Carolina Infantry. A year later in April 1862 Henry received a promotion to sergeant and several weeks later moved up to third lieutenant. Levi would remain a private in the company for the duration of his service.

Even though their Civil War experiences were somewhat different, the two brothers had an unfortunate similarity to take home to North Carolina. During the early days of July 1863 both men were participating in the Battle of Gettysburg. During the fighting Levi was severely wounded in the left leg and captured. The leg was damaged to the point where amputation was necessary. After his leg was removed, Levi was transferred to a prison hospital at David's Island in New York City Harbor.

Brother Henry made it through the Battle of Gettysburg without a scratch. However, on July 13, during the retreat to Virginia he too was severely wounded in the left leg and captured. Henry's leg, just like his brother Levi's, was damaged to the point that it had to be amputated. He was taken to a hospital in Baltimore and eventually transferred to Johnson's Island, a prison for Confederate officers on Lake Erie.

For both men the fighting war was over. They were both paroled and eventually made their way back home to North Carolina. Levi quit farming to be a merchant in Charlotte while Henry became a physician in Huntersville.[11]

Before and after the war photos of brothers Henry J. and Levi J. Walker who both lost their left legs during the Gettysburg Campaign.

Confederate Veteran

The story of the two men losing their left legs during the Gettysburg campaign is not the only thing that they shared. Both legs were amputated just below the knee—the cuts so close that the two brothers were able to exchange wooden legs and still have a perfect fit.[12]

A Penny Carved

Camp life during the Civil War was at times very dull. The actual amount of time soldiers spent in camp was much greater than on campaign or in battle. To relieve the monotony, soldiers had to devise ways to occupy the long hours. One way to pass the time was to make handicrafts using a variety of materials. The men made pipes from clay, cobs, or brier root to pass the time. They carved rings from shells and bone and whittled and carved other objects from wood found around the camp.[13]

At times these crafted items were somewhat bizarre or at least peculiar. In the book *Strange Tales of the Civil War* it was related that Sergeant Major George Polley of the 10th Massachusetts Volunteers occupied some of his time by carving his own headboard (grave stone) out of the wooden top of a cracker box just hours before he was killed.[14] There were also reportings of jewelry being fashioned out of human bones, particularly bones from dead enemy soldiers.

One place to find these products of long, lonely hours of camp life was on the battlefield. Men frequently lost them during action only to have them picked up by another soldier as a souvenir of the engagement. One such item of handicraft was found by Private William Milford of Company H, 23rd Pennsylvania Volunteers. It was during the Battle of Gettysburg, while lying behind a breastwork on Culp's Hill that Private Milford found the head of a penny. Apparently someone had busied themselves by cutting out the rim of the penny and possibly dropped the head or threw it away. It was indeed a very odd item to find on any battlefield.

Private Milford kept the penny head in his pocket as a souvenir. Several months later he was engaged in a conversation with Lieutenant William Vodges of Company F. As the two men spoke, Private Milford took the penny head out of his pocket to show the lieutenant. A stunned Lieutenant Vodges replied at seeing the relic, "Why, Milford, you are the man I have been looking for." The lieutenant then proceeded to reach into his pocket and pulled out the rim of a penny with the head cut out. The two men put the pieces together for a perfect fit. Lieutenant Vodges explained he had found his part of the penny when the regiment had gone from Culp's Hill to the center of the Union Line near Major General George Meade's headquarters on July 3.

The lieutenant gave his portion of the penny to Private Milford. Years later in 1886 when the veterans of the 23rd Pennsylvania dedicated their monument on Culp's Hill, Private Milford donated the two pieces of the penny to be included in a box of other regimental artifacts that was placed in the base of the monument.[15]

Not So Dead After All

The people of Fond du Lac, Wisconsin, were shocked when they heard the news that Lieutenant Colonel Edward Bragg was dead. A telegram to his wife told the story that Lieutenant Colonel Edward Bragg was killed on September 17, 1862, in action during the Battle of Antietam. The telegram, from a sergeant of Company I, 6th Wisconsin

Lieutenant Colonel Edward Bragg was not killed at Antietam but went on to be promoted to brigadier general.

MOLLUS-MASS Coll. at USAMHI

Volunteers, stated that the body would be shipped home to Fond du Lac. Immediately the city council convened and began making funeral arrangements for the local hero. A committee was selected to travel to Chicago and intercept the body to escort it home.

When the committee arrived in Chicago they were stunned to find that the body of Lieutenant Colonel Bragg was not there or anywhere nearby. Instead the body they gazed upon was Captain Edwin A. Brown, another resident of Fond du Lac and member of the 6th Wisconsin. Somewhere someone was confused as to who died and who survived.

The Battle of Antietam was a nightmare for those engaged. The experience of the men of the 6th Wisconsin was no exception. During the morning of September 17 the men of the 6th were deployed into a line of battle and moving forward toward the David Miller farm buildings. The right flank of the regiment rested on the Sharpsburg and Hagerstown Turnpike. As the left flank of the regiment moved forward, they were obstructed by a picket fence around the Millers' garden. The order was given to pull the fence down but the men were unable to remove the obstruction. The men were then instructed to pass through a gate in the fence. Major

Rufus Dawes recorded what happened next: "Here Captain Edwin A. Brown, of company 'E,' was instantly killed. There is in my mind as I write the spectacle of a young officer, with uplifted sword, shouting in a loud imperative voice the order I had given him, 'Company "E," on the right by file into line!' A bullet passes into his open mouth, and the voice is forever silent."

The regiment pushed on toward the now famous Farmer Miller Cornfield. On the right flank a volley was received from a Confederate battle line in a woods. During this first volley Lieutenant Colonel Edward Bragg was hit. Keeping his senses, he quickly ordered the men to change fronts and form behind the turnpike fence facing the new threat. He then sent an orderly to seek out Major Dawes who was farther on the left in the cornfield. Dawes described what he saw when arriving at Colonel Bragg's side, "I saw a tear in his overcoat which he had on. I feared that he was shot through the body. I called two men from the ranks, who bundled him quickly into a shelter tent, and hurried away with him."[16]

Major Dawes' worst fears were not realized. Colonel Bragg received a "slight but painful wound in the left arm."[17] He eventually returned to duty and was promoted to the rank of brigadier general in June 1864. After the war he was active in politics including being elected to the United States Congress. It was not until June 1912 that the citizens of Fond du Lac were able to rightly mourn the passing of Edward Bragg.[18] Captain Edwin Brown's body was taken back to Fond du Lac by the committee and was bestowed the same respect by the town elders that had been planned for Lieutenant Colonel Edward Bragg.[19]

A Tribute to Grant

Some of the most valued relics of the Civil War are battle flags. Used as a symbol of each regiment the flags soon became a source of pride for the soldiers they represented. To lose a flag in battle was a source of humiliation to the regiment. To capture an enemy's flag was a cause for promotion and commendation. After the war many of the states collected their regimental flags and placed them on display. The Massachusetts flags were no exception. Placed in stands and wrapped with silken cords, the battle flags were displayed in the state capitol building in Boston. There they stood in their place of honor.[20]

In July 1885 news traveled throughout the country that General Ulysses S. Grant had died.[21] Across the nation people mourned the passing of one of the key figures of the war and a former president. Flags were lowered to half-staff and veterans stopped and saluted as church bells tolled. Outside the state capitol building in Boston guns were fired every minute. Massachusetts was saying good-bye to a hero. Inside the capitol building the vibrations from the blasts loosened the silken cords that had already rotted with age. As the cords fell away, the battle-torn flags that had waved so defiantly twenty years before bowed and tilted forward as if saluting the passing of the dead general.[22]

Chapter Four

Ironies

An Odd Name for a Battle

By early spring of 1862 the Civil War had completed its first year. Casualties had already risen higher than most people could have ever imagined when the war began. Major engagements had been fought at Bull Run, Wilson's Creek, and Pea Ridge. However, that April the war took a turn for the worse near a little country church named Shiloh. Located near the Tennessee River the Shiloh Church was a place where marriages and baptisms were performed, where lives were changed and people found peace. But during April 6 and 7, 1862, over 23,000 men were either killed or wounded here. For everyone in the battle their lives were altered forever and no one found peace.[1] In a letter to his wife, Brigadier General James Garfield described his feelings after walking over the battlefield, "The horrible sights that I have witnessed on this field I can never describe. No blaze of glory, that flashes around the magnificent triumphs of war, can ever atone for the unwritten and unutterable horrors of the scene of carnage."[2]

With 23,000 casualties the Battle of Shiloh was the worst engagement to date of the Civil War. Its casualty list was greater than all previous battles combined. But Shiloh would also

The Shiloh Church, around which the bloody Battle of Shiloh was fought.
MOLLUS-MASS Coll. at USAMHI

mark a turning point that made all the former battles seem like child's play. Still to come would be three more years of bloodshed at places like Chancellorsville, Gettysburg, and the Wilderness. Casualty lists would outgrow anyone's imagination as the slaughter continued.

Ironically, it was around this small church that the nightmare of civil war would truly begin to emerge. How unfitting that it occur near a place named Shiloh, the biblical interpretation meaning "place of peace."[3]

If the Name Fits, Fight

By September 1863 the nation realized the price of war was to be high. On the 19th and 20th the Union Army of the Cumberland and Confederate Army of Tennessee met along Chickamauga Creek just across the Georgia state line from Chattanooga, Tennessee. For two days the armies engaged in brutal combat. During the afternoon of the second day Federal troops fled to Chattanooga, leaving the field to the Southern victor. In the end 34,624 men or 28 percent were killed, wounded or missing.[4]

Ironically the location of such a bloody affair is suitable when one examines the name *Chickamauga* and its history. Years prior to the bloody struggle of September 1863 another struggle took place along banks of the Chickamauga. In the days before European settlers moved west of the Appalachian Mountains the banks of Chickamauga Creek were home to the Cherokee, a native American tribe who had called this land home for hundreds of years. However, in the late 1700s intruders from the east appeared as white settlers moved west from the Atlantic Coast. Along with the settlers came doom for the Cherokee in the dreaded disease small pox. Having no natural immunity and no adequate medicines, the Cherokee, like other Native American people, easily succumbed to the disease and thousands died. In order to relieve their suffering, victims of the epidemic fled to the creek and its cool water; but still no relief was found and the banks of the Chickamauga became littered with the bodies of the dead. It is thus very fitting that the Cherokee named the creek Chickamauga or "River of Death."[5]

A Grave Situation

In November 1861 both Union and Confederate forces were trying to gain a foothold in the border state of Kentucky. During part of this maneuvering the 33rd Indiana Infantry was ordered to retreat from its position at London to Crab Orchard. The column set out at 10 o'clock on the night of November 13. Shortly after the movement started ". . . a cold, dreary rain began to fall in torrents. The road soon became almost impassable, and the mountain streams were swollen in volume to and beyond their banks. The march continued all through the night, and when daylight came a most deplorable scene presented itself, which gradually assumed more aggravated forms. Wagons were stuck in the mud, and the mules had given way to sheer exhaustion." In the command of the 33rd were one hundred eighty men that had been taken from a hospital and loaded into open wagons for the forty-mile trek. Already sick, the rain-soaked men were now in dire straits.[6] As the column approached Mount Vernon the toll of the exposure to the harsh elements became unbearable. To relieve this suffering, several men had to be left at the home of a local Union man named Judge Kirtley.

Among the men were John M. Estis and Corporal W. J. Knox of Company C who were left at the home to act as nurses for the ailing men. The remainder of the column proceeded to Crab Orchard, reaching that destination after two days' travel. The effects on the regiment were disastrous with the sick reaching a staggering 250 men.

After ten days at Crab Orchard Private David P. Robb of Company F persuaded his colonel to allow him to travel back to Mount Vernon and pay a visit to the men left behind at Judge Kirtley's home. Ailing from the cold and rain Private Robb was welcomed by his fellow soldiers. However, several days later Private Robb's condition worsened and he soon died. Estis, who was still feeling poorly, traveled to a local cemetery and proceeded to dig a grave for his fallen comrade. During the process of lowering the body of Private Robb into the ground a detail arrived from Crab Orchard. The burial was stopped and a beautiful metallic coffin acquired for the body which was then shipped home to Princeton, Indiana. Sadly for Estis his struggle to dig the grave had strained his already weak body. He relapsed and soon died. Ironically, a fresh grave was available. The same grave he had dug for his friend would now be occupied by Estis himself.[7]

Orders His Own Execution

The night of April 18, 1862, was dark. Captain Abram Wood of Company C, 4th Michigan Volunteers, was posting pickets on his front for the night.[8] The 4th Michigan was part of the Union army that had been besieging Yorktown, Virginia, since April 5.

During the posting of the last picket Captain Wood gave strict orders to "shoot the first man who approaches from the direction of the rebels, without waiting to ask for the countersign." Satisfied, the captain started back to camp. As the night was dark the captain soon became disoriented. Once he realized he had been walking toward the Confederate defenses, he promptly turned around. Unfortunately, for Captain Wood he walked straight toward his last picket. Without a warning the picket shot and Captain Wood fell mortally wounded.[9]

No Guns Allowed

On the morning of July 1, 1863, the quiet southern Pennsylvania town of Gettysburg became the scene of what would be one of the greatest battles in history. Early in the battle Union cavalry was able to stall the advance of Confederate infantry. But as the day wore and reinforcements gathered on both sides, Confederates forces coming from Carlisle were able to rout the Union XI Corps positioned north of the town. With the XI Corps on the run the Union I Corps was compelled to retreat from their position on the west side of the town. As the two Union corps retreated through Gettysburg, their destination was the high ground around the town cemetery.

The Evergreen Cemetery was the last resting place for many citizens of Gettysburg, including the town's namesake, James Gettys.[10] Established in 1856, one of its most noted and photographed features was the arched gatehouse that faced the Baltimore Pike.[11] It was in this cemetery that the residents of Gettysburg spent time in peaceful remembrance of their loved ones. However, on this day the quiet and peacefulness was broken by the fury of war. The hollow ground would soon become a focal point of the battle. Men from

The gatehouse of Gettysburg's Evergreen Cemetery as it looked just days after the battle.

MOLLUS-MASS Coll. at USAMHI

broken regiments would find shelter there from the day's fighting. As the afternoon turned into night, artillery batteries were quickly placed into position to repel any Confederate assault. In all about forty-six cannon of different caliber were posted in and around the cemetery.[12]

With all the traffic from the thousands of men and guns the sacred ground was quickly turned into a mere shadow of its former self. The next day, July 2, one soldier wrote of the scene, "a beautiful cemetery it was, but now is trodden down, laid a waste, desecrated. The fences are all down, the many graves have been run over, beautiful lots with iron fences and splendid monuments have been destroyed or soiled, and our infantry and artillery occupy those sacred grounds where the dead are sleeping. . . ."[13]

Ironically, a sign had been posted on the cemetery grounds warning that "Driving, riding and shooting on these grounds strictly prohibited. Any person violating this ordinance will be punished by fine and imprisonment."[14]

For the next three days the town ordinance was temporarily rescinded. Nobody was fined or imprisoned but many men did pay the ultimate price with their lives. The Evergreen Cemetery survived the battle and has become one of Gettysburg's most important landmarks.

Chapter Five

Dreams

Fighting in His Sleep

There is little wonder why men during the Civil War would have had nightmares. With the horrific battles fought by day many men certainly relived this action when they were finally able to close their eyes for a little rest. One soldier who had such a problem was thirty-three-year-old Sergeant Samuel Fletcher of Company I, 9th New Hampshire Volunteers. Sergeant Fletcher was only in the service for one month when he had his first experience of battle at South Mountain and then Antietam.[1] It wasn't until three months later in December when he experienced his next battle. This one occurred in his sleep and was more hazardous than the previous two.

Taking his trusty rifle to sleep with him, Sergeant Fletcher had a dream that night that turned into a nightmare that became all too real. It is not known what he dreamt or what demons he encountered. But, back and forth he fought with some unknown enemy in the depth of his sleep. Maybe the horrors of Antietam had come back to haunt his subconscious, or the thought of some future battle awakened his fear.

Whatever stirred in his sleepy mind was frightening enough to cause Sergeant Fletcher to struggle. Unfortunately the only thing within his grasp was a loaded rifle. As the struggle grew more violent he accidentally discharged the gun. Sleeping men within earshot of the rifle fire were suddenly awakened. Grabbing their weapons the drowsy men responded to what they thought was a night attack. Upon reaching the scene they discovered that there were no rebels lurking in the darkness, instead the only casualty was Sergeant Fletcher lying on the ground crying out in pain. During the imaginary fight Sergeant Fletcher had shot himself in the foot when his gun accidentally discharged.[2] It was to be his last battle. The foot wound ended Sergeant Fletcher's Civil war career and on January 1, 1863, he was discharged for disability.[3]

Dreamed of Murder

It is not uncommon to have dreams. Many people have several dreams each night while they sleep. These dreams usually consist of events of the past several days or thoughts that are weighing heavily on a person's mind. Many times the dream is a conglomeration of recent events that forms some type of absurd storyline forgotten by the next morning. However, some dreams, as odd as they may be, are hard to erase from memory. Especially those dealing with future events. Such was the case of Private Edward Blain of the 113th Ohio Volunteers.

The 113th belonged to the XIV Corps of the Army of the Cumberland. During the winter of 1864–65 they participated in General William T. Sherman's famous March to the Sea.[4] By February, the 113th was in South Carolina heading north. On the 24th of the month they crossed to the north side of the Catawba River. Private Blain had never been near this area of the country. However, he was oddly familiar with his surroundings: the river crossing, the hill on the other shore, and the house that stood on its crest. He had seen it all months before in a dream.

In the dream he climbed to the top of the hill where the house stood. However, at this point the dream turned into a nightmare when the sleeping Blain witnessed a murder. Now the scene was set for the dream to be played out—only this time it was real.

After crossing the river, the 113th stacked their arms for the night and made camp. Upon completing his duties, Private Blain, possibly curious about his dream, climbed to the top of the nearby hill where the house stood. There, exactly as in his dream he had months earlier, he arrived just in time to witness George Workman of Company B being fatally shot by an insane soldier. Sadly Private Blain was unable to stop or even change the events foretold in his dream. Instead he was destined to be a player in the drama, but having no say in its outcome.[5]

Saw It in His Dream

On the morning of December 29, 1862, Captain Casper Schleich of Company F, 55th Illinois Infantry, joined his men for breakfast. Nearby flowed the Yazoo River, a branch of the Mississippi. In their front lay Chickasaw Bayou, a formidable swamp that obstructed the Union army's advance on the city of Vicksburg. It was this swamp that would be the focus of the day's activities for Captain Schleich and the men of the 55th Illinois.

As Captain Schleich rose from his breakfast he remarked to the men, "Boys, I am glad I ate with you this morning, for I am going out here to be killed by these rebels, and I want you to bear witness that I desire to be buried here on this sand ridge." It was a startling revelation to the men of Company F, but for Captain Schleich it was all too real. Days earlier he had witnessed his own death in a dream while staying in Memphis. The morning after the dream he confided to Milton Haney, chaplain of the regiment, "I dreamed that I stood facing a rebel about fifty yards away when he shot me through the heart . . ."

Captain Schleich was well liked by the men of the regiment. In the regimental history of the 55th it was written that he had ". . . few equals in intellect and all those qualities which form true manhood."[6] Having enlisted when the regiment was originally formed in August 1861, Schleich was mustered in as a second lieutenant in Company A, which became known as the Canton Blues. Less than a year later, on July 1, 1862, he was transferred to Company F and awarded a promotion to captain.

Even after having such a frightening dream he did not stumble in his duties and prepared for the assault on the Confederate line. On this day the objective of the 55th Illinois along with the remainder of the Second Division was to cross the Chickasaw Bayou. While crossing the swampy ground the men from Illinois would be faced with Confederate artillery and small arms fire. Making the matter more difficult was the fact that the crossing would take place along a narrow sand bar, allowing only a limited number of troops to make the assault at one time. In addition the Confederate defenses were well designed. "On the side of the Federals this

Chickasaw Bayou where Captain Casper Schleich dreamed he would be killed.

MOLLUS-MASS Coll. at USAMHI

crossing was protected by an abatis of thickly fallen timber, the interlocked trunks and limbs being covered with festoons of Spanish moss. On the opposite side was an impracticable bank, surmounted by a levee, which formed a perfect parapet for the foe."[7]

Before attempting to cross the sand bar the abatis would have to be removed. This became the mission of the 54th Ohio. While the abatis was being cleared, the 55th would serve on the skirmish line to retard as much as possible any Confederate fire.

For several hours Union gunners used twenty-pound Parrott guns to help clear the Confederate fortifications. As the guns pounded the defenses, the men of the 55th Illinois watched and waited for their turn at the day's work. Early in the afternoon the 54th Ohio was ordered to remove the abatis from the sandbar. With that order the deadly task of the 55th Illinois began. By companies the Illinois men spread out among the logs and began to fire at any Confederates foolish enough to show their heads.[8]

When the time came for the men of Company F to take their place in line, Captain Schleich prepared to lead them forward. Before joining the skirmish line, Chaplain Haney spoke to Captain Schleich and cautioned him about the enemy fire. After the words were spoken between the two men, Captain Schleich, resigned to his fate, moved forward to take his position where he would direct the attack.[9] "A few rods brought him within the circle of danger, but he walked fearlessly at the head of his men, the very impersonation of soldierly valor." The captain barely made it to the skirmish line when "with his arm outstretched for the purpose of directing one of his followers to a place of safety . . . he was struck fair in the breast by a bullet . . ."[10] Falling into the arms of Sergeant Henry Haney, Captain Schleich cried, "I am shot."[11]

It was just as he had dreamed. A rebel sharpshooter's bullet found its mark and Captain Schleich passed into eternity. At the end of the day the assault failed and the 55th had lost one of its finest sons.

Death Foretold in A Dream

The Battle of Fredericksburg was a nightmare for many of the men, both North and South, who witnessed its slaughter. It was a cold day in December 1862 when wave after wave of Union troops assaulted the Confederate positions on the heights south of the town. In the end the battle was a disaster for the Northern cause with a total of 12,700 Union and 5,300 Southern troops victims of the carnage.[12]

For Private William J. Dennis the battle truly was a horrible dream. Private Dennis was a member of the Jeff Davis Artillery that was formed in Selma, Alabama. The battery saw limited action that cold December day, being held in reserve until two o'clock in the afternoon. At that time one section of guns was ordered forward to the eastern end of the battlefield. Here they took up position near Hamilton's Crossing and began a cannonade with Union batteries across the Rappahannock River. The return fire from the Union guns caused its share of destruction to the Alabamian battery.[13] Private John Crosby "was struck by a solid shot and mashed into a pulp, the shot passing entirely through his body as he lay on the ground."[14] Corporal Edward W. Nobles fared much better, receiving a serious foot wound but was saved from the grave. The third casualty of the day was Private Dennis who also received a serious foot wound during the artillery duel.[15]

Private Dennis knew when the battery went into action that day that it would have very serious consequences for him. Two nights prior to the battle he dreamt that he would be killed. He revealed his despair to John Purifay the next day while the battery was waiting to be called to a forward position. Purifay had questioned Dennis about his health. Private Dennis replied, "I am feeling rather sad, Jack. I had a dream last night which impressed me very much. I dreamed I had been in battle and was killed, and in spirit form was wandering about in space, when I met John Crosby, who also seemed to be in spirit form, having been killed before I was." Purifay tried to comfort his depressed friend, telling him that dreams really did not have any meaning and that he would be fine.

As the battle raged and the Jeff Davis Artillery was called into action, Private Dennis could only have assumed his nightmare was about to come true. But now it seemed as if he was wrong. Indeed Private Crosby was killed just like he had dreamt. But for Private Dennis the consequence of battle was a foot wound, something generally not considered to be a death blow.

After suffering the wound, Private Dennis was taken to a surgeon who amputated his foot. However, the dream was not to be denied. Instead of escaping his fate of death at Fredericksburg, Private Dennis' dream did come true. Complications from his foot wound set in and he died on January 19, 1863.[16]

An Amusing Slumber

One dream that had to certainly be amusing for those who witnessed it occurred on Johnson's Island in Sandusky Bay on Lake Erie. Johnson's Island was home to a Union prison that housed around 4,200 Confederate officers. The winter of 1863–64 was severe enough to cause Sandusky Bay to freeze, allowing Johnson's Island to be reached by foot. Thus the 23rd Pennsylvania Volunteers was sent to the island to guard against any rebel attacks from across the ice. The assignment was welcomed by the men. It was a well-deserved rest from the rigors of campaigning with the Army of the Potomac. Johnson's Island had "comfortable quarters, plenty of rations, camp fires every night in the barracks . . ."[17]

Among the soldiers of Company F were James and Peter Henry who slept together in an upper berth. The night was quiet as the tired soldiers tried to get some much-needed sleep. Suddenly the silence was broken by the sounds of a scuffle. A

cry of "murder: get a light, he, cut my throat" was heard in the darkness. The sleeping soldiers quickly awakened and immediately struck a light. The men rushed to the scene of the noise curious as to what had disturbed their slumber. To their amazement they found Peter Henry standing with his hands around his own neck exclaiming that James Henry had cut his throat. In the dim light of the night a dark liquid could be seen on the

While dreaming, James Henry attempted to cut another soldier's throat with an ink bottle.

History of the Twenty-Third Pennsylvania

victim's neck. However, upon inspection of the "wound" it was found that there was no blood. Instead the dark liquid was ink.

The men quickly surmised what had happened. It seems that James had a habit of walking in his sleep. While on his nightly stroll he dreamed of being captured and while attempting to escape grabbed Peter. In the struggle that ensued James secured a bottle of ink from a nearby shelf and proceeded to use it like a knife to cut Peter's throat. At this time Peter awoke with the ink splashing onto his neck. Peter naturally thought his throat was being slashed. It was then that he rolled out of bed onto the floor to secure his escape and cried for help. Ironically, for Peter Henry the reprieve from the Army of the Potomac to the comfortable quarters of Johnson's Island wasn't as safe and secure as he certainly would have liked.[18]

Chapter Six

The Big Guns

A Shot for Hill

During the Battle of Antietam in September 1862 thousands of artillery rounds were fired causing massive amounts of destruction to lives and property. Most of the time the victims of such fire did not have the opportunity to witness the source of their impending doom. However, one incident did occur when witnesses were able to see the gun fired and literally trace the shell to its final impact.

During a lull in the fighting, Generals Robert E. Lee, James Longstreet, and Daniel Harvey Hill were riding along the Boonsboro Pike. Desiring to have a better view of the events on the field the generals decided to climb a hill. Lee and Longstreet dismounted in order to become inconspicuous to Union gunners who were looking for targets. As the men started toward the crest of the hill, Longstreet noticed that Hill was still astride his horse. Looking at the mounted general he remarked, "If you insist on riding up there and drawing the fire, give us a little interval so that we may not be in the line of the fire when they open upon you."[1]

On the other side of Antietam Creek, about a mile distant, was positioned Battery I of the 5th United States

Artillery commanded by Captain Stephen H. Weed.[2] During the temporary lull on the battlefield Captain Weed searched for something to shoot at. Looking through his field glasses he spied the group of generals on the crest of the hill near the Boonsboro Pike. Even though he probably had no idea of the high-valued target he had in his sights, Captain Weed took this as a great opportunity for target practice. Carefully he sighted the gun and pulled the lanyard, sending the shell on its deadly mission.

Back on the crest of the hill the generals surveyed the field. While looking through his field glasses General Longstreet noticed a puff of white smoke coming from one of the Union cannon across the creek. Turning to the stubborn Hill, who was still mounted, he said, "There is a shot for you." Three or four seconds passed since Captain Weed had fired his cannon

at the group of generals. Still watching from the crest of the hill the three men heard the whistle of the cannon ball. Then suddenly it struck its target, shattering the front legs of Hill's horse. The animal fell down upon the stumps of its legs with Hill still mounted. Captain Weed's target practice had proved to be right on the mark. For Hill it was the second close call of the day. Earlier he had another horse shot beneath him.[3]

General Daniel Harvey Hill became a target for Union gunners when he refused to dismount from his horse.

MOLLUS-MASS Coll. at USAMHI

This is one of those incidents in history where luck plays a major role. Had Captain Weed's aim been any more precise, General Hill would have been lost to the Confederate cause. Quite possibly had the gun been moved by a hair, Generals Longstreet and Lee may have been lost, certainly changing the course of history.

Landing in His Lap

According to General James Longstreet the best shot ever fired by an artilleryman was fired by a Confederate gunner during the siege of Yorktown, Virginia. Yorktown is located near the tip of the Virginia peninsula. Cutting across the peninsula is the Warwick River providing a natural defensive line. Behind the Warwick, Southern troops constructed defensive works and a line of artillery batteries all designed to slow down the Federal advance on Richmond. One of these batteries was stationed near a grist mill named Wynn's Mill. It was near this mill that Longstreet witnessed an amazing shot.

On April 21, 1862, Longstreet observed a Union officer opposite the Confederate lines set up a plane table. He then proceeded to sit down to draw a map of the Confederate defenses. The officer's name was First Lieutenant Orlando G. Wagner of the Topographical Engineers Army of the Potomac.[4]

Nearby in the Confederate works the men of the Richmond Howitzers also watched Lieutenant Wagner with interest. However, they also saw this as a challenge. How dare this Union officer boldly sit down in plain view and draw a map of their lines. Corporal Holzburton of the Second Company quickly determined how to deal with this display of arrogance. He took it upon himself to sight one of the company's ten-pound Parrott rifles at the Union officer. Satisfied with his aim, Corporal Holzburton pulled the lanyard of the gun, sending the shell on its way. Seconds later the shot hit its mark, landing directly on the table where Lieutenant Wagner was working. It was truly a remarkable shot, possibly one in a million. However, for Lieutenant Wagner his map-making days were over as the shot inflicted a mortal wound.[5]

Spiked Gun at Gettysburg

One of the most remarkable incidents of accuracy firing a cannon occurred during the first day of the Battle of Gettysburg. During the early afternoon hours, Battery I of the 1st Ohio Light Artillery was positioned with its six light twelve-pound cannon between the Taneytown and Baltimore Roads.[6] In this position just north of the town of Gettysburg, the Union XI Corps was preparing to encounter Confederates just arriving from Carlisle.

An artillery duel soon developed between the Ohio guns and a Confederate battery of twelve pounders commanded by Captain Richard Page.[7] The first shot fired from one of the 1st Ohio's guns was high and harmlessly flew over the heads of the enemy cannon. In response to the miss a cheer arose from the Confederate line. Unhappy with the first round, commander of the 1st Ohio guns, Captain Hubert Dilger, stepped forward and personally sighted the next shot. The round scored a direct hit, dismounting one of the rebel twelve pounders and killing its horses. Elated by this success, Captain Dilger proceeded to sight a second gun. However, this time there was no visible effect to the dissatisfaction of the Union commander who quickly voiced his opinion.

Nearby Colonel Philip Brown of the 157th New York Volunteers heard the angry words. With his regiment directly behind and supporting the 1st Ohio Battery he watched with interest the artillery exchange through his field glasses. Hearing Captain Dilger voice his disappointment at the missed shot he quickly disagreed and yelled to the Ohio artilleryman, "What effect, Captain Dilger?" The artillery captain was dismayed by Colonel Brown's enthusiasm and quickly took a look through his field glasses. He was astonished by what he saw and replied, "I have spiked a gun for them, plugging it at the muzzle."

Captain Dilger's aim during the second shot was so accurate that the ball from the Union gun hit the rebel cannon square in the muzzle, lodging itself in the opening. With the ball stuck in the Confederate cannon's mouth the gun was unusable until it could be repaired—something that was not going to happen for some time.

It would be hard to cal-

Captain Hubert Dilger fired the perfect shot during the first day at Gettysburg.

MOLLUS-MASS Coll. at USAMHI

culate the odds of such an occurrence happening. Just hitting a gun with a ball would be considered to be a great shot. This would be equivalent to Robin Hood splitting an arrow with another arrow. Captain Dilger could truly say that he could never do that again even if he tried.[8]

Another Spiked Gun

A similar incident took place two days later, at Gettsyburg, during Longstreet's famous assault upon the center of the Union line. At about one o'clock in the afternoon Confederate artillery began shelling the center of the Union line along Cemetery Ridge in preparation for the assault.[9] Union Brigadier General Francis Walker described the scene in his *History of the Second Army Corps*, "The air shrieked with flying shot, the bursting shells sent their deadly fragments down in showers upon the rocky ridge and over the plain behind; the earth was thrown up in clouds of dust as the monstrous missiles buried themselves in the ground, or glanced from the surface to take a new and, perchance, more fatal flight; on every hand caissons exploded, struck by iron balls which but a half-minute before had lain in the limber-chests of batteries a mile away."[10]

Finally, after ten to fifteen minutes Union batteries were ordered to open fire upon their Confederate counterparts. Union gunners rushed to their positions and readied their guns to return fire. It wasn't long until the whole Union line was ablaze.

Battery B of the 1st Rhode Island Light Artillery was positioned just left of the now famous copse of trees. The Rhode Islanders worked feverishly to man their four Napoleon cannons as Confederate shells fell thick and fast all around. But then disaster struck. Privates William Jones and Alfred Gardner were in the process of placing a round in the muzzle of gun number four when a rebel shell scored a direct hit. The shell slammed into the muzzle of the gun and exploded. Jones lost part of his head to the blast and died immediately. Gardner had his left arm almost completely torn

Private Alfred G. Gardner of the 1st Rhode Island Artillery was killed when a shell struck gun number four.

Battery B First R.I. Light Artillery

Sergeant Albert Straight failed to load gun number four of Battery B, 1st Rhode Island Artillery, when a Confederate shell dented the muzzle.

Battery B First R.I. Light Artillery

off at the shoulder. He lingered between life and death for several minutes. His tent mate Sergeant Albert Straight rushed to the dying man's side. Gardner requested of his friend that he send his Bible home to his wife and tell her he died happy. With that Gardner shouted, "Glory to God!" and died.

Corporal James Dye and Straight took control of the gun. Sergeant Straight attempted to force another round into the tube but the Confederate shell had dented the muzzle. The two men then tried to force the ball down the barrel with the rammer, but to no avail. With the ball halfway in and halfway out of the muzzle, an axe was procured to pound the projectile in farther. But before it could be used, another shell struck the wheel of the gun, finally putting it out of commission. The gun was abandoned with the ball still lodged in its muzzle. Eventually a third round struck the trail of the cannon, killing John Green.

The disabled gun number four of Battery B, 1st Rhode Island Light Artillery, with the ball still lodged in its muzzle.

Battery B First R.I. Light Artillery

Slowly the heat from the barrel dissipated, shrinking the muzzle even tighter around the stuck ball.[11] During the third day at Gettysburg the gun was hit three times by shot or shell and an additional thirty-nine times by musket balls.[12]

The gun was spiked at the muzzle and no longer any use as a weapon of war. Instead it was to be used as a tribute to Rhode Island's sacrifice to the cause of freedom. The gun would be ever after known as the "Gettysburg Gun" and was presented to the state of Rhode Island by the United States Congress in 1874. It was kept in storage until 1903 when on Battle Flag Day (October 17) the 12-pound Napoleon was moved to the New State House in Providence and placed on public display.

Log Mortars

There were times during the Civil War when both sides had to be resourceful in order to gain an advantage over their opponent. One of these methods was the use of Quaker guns. Of course, like the name implies, these guns were not used to kill, merely to deceive the enemy into thinking they were real cannons. Thus, being merely fakes, they could be made out of almost anything that resembled a cannon barrel from a distance. General James Longstreet in his memoirs wrote that immediately after the First Battle of Bull Run his troops "collected a number of old wagon-wheels and mounted on them stove-pipes of different caliber, till we had formidable-looking batteries."[13] Logs that had been painted black and placed in cannon emplacements were also used. Simple but effective Quaker guns are generally thought to have been used by Confederate forces due to the lack of war materials and money. However, Union forces were also not too proud to use a similar weapon. The difference was the Union guns were used to kill, not to deceive.

It was during the siege of Vicksburg when Major General Ulysses S. Grant's Union Army of the Tennessee employed a unique type of weapon. During the siege that lasted from May 18 through July 4, 1863, the Federal army had a limited amount of siege artillery.[14] One type of gun in short supply was mortars. These weapons are designed to hurl a projectile in a high arc, enabling gunners to throw shells over wall fortifications. Since it would take time to have the mortars delivered, Union engineers came up with an innovative idea. They would build their own mortars at the scene. The only problem was they did not have the facilities and equipment to forge such weaponry out of iron. Instead the engineers looked at the materials at

Quaker guns were used to mislead the opposing armies into thinking defensive works were fortified with heavy guns.

MOLLUS-MASS Coll. at USAMHI

hand and decided to try to manufacture their mortars out of a material that was in plentiful supply—wood.

The engineers cut down large-diameter hardwood trees. They then sawed the logs to length and bored holes in the center to accept a six- or twelve-pound shell. The log was reinforced with iron bands and the mortar complete.[15] It was a simple operation, for the mortar balls only had to be thrown a short distance up and over the rebel fortifications. There was no need for a serious amount of velocity since the balls would explode with a timed fuse.

The whole idea of making mortar tubes from wooden logs seems to be ridiculous, but oddly enough the experiment worked. The wooden mortars didn't work as well as regular iron guns but they served the purpose. It was reported that the homemade wooden mortars "stood firing well and

Log mortars were used during the siege of Vicksburg.
Battles and Leaders of the Civil War

gave sufficiently good results at 100 or 150 yards."[16] Crude
but effective Yankee ingenuity.

Justice Is Served

Henry J. Savage of Company G, 1st Delaware Infantry,
had been in many of the major engagements of the Army of
the Potomac. During this time he had witnessed more than
his share of horrors. However, in his latter years as a resident
in the Soldier's Home in Milwaukee, Wisconsin, one incident
stood out in his mind that was more terrible than all the rest.

It was during the Battle of Antietam on September 17,
1862, that Henry Savage witnessed the sight he couldn't forget. The 1st Delaware was involved in the assaults near the
center of the Confederate line, better known as the Bloody
Lane. The fighting was so horrible at this position that it was

said a person could walk from one end of the Bloody Lane to the other without touching the earth but instead stepping on the bodies of the dead and dying. During one of the attacks Savage was wounded and ordered to the rear. While making his way to receive medical attention, he came across a man stumbling about the field. His arms were held out as he wandered to and fro as if searching for something in the dark. Both his eyes had been shot out and he was begging for someone to kill him and put him out of his misery. Sadly this was not an odd sight on a battlefield where so many men were in agony beyond belief. One moment a man is perfectly capable of seeing all the wonders of the world and in the next moment pain and darkness enter his life.

While observing this sad situation, Savage noticed a lieutenant from the 4th New York Infantry walk up to the blind man and cruelly inquire if he really meant what he said. The blinded man quickly agreed that he wanted to die. In such a dire situation most mortals would beg for mercy but only out of the need for pity and attention.

However, the lieutenant wasn't about to provide any pity. He simply pulled out his pistol and placed the barrel to the unfortunate man's head and fired. The blind man immediately fell to the ground dead, his agony over. What possibly startled Savage more than the cruel and heartless judgment of the lieutenant was what happened next. Immediately, as the lieutenant returned his pistol to its holster he exclaimed, "It was better thus for the poor fellow could —," but never finished his statement. It was as if a power from above passed judgment, when a solid shot smashed into his head.[17]

Chapter Seven

Dumb Luck

Freak Accidents Happen

Freak accidents happen from time to time—at home, in the workplace, or while playing a favorite sport. When they occur during wartime these accidents are usually deadly. Sergeant Rufus Dooley of the 21st Indiana recalled an incident during the siege of Port Hudson, Louisiana, that occurred from May 24 through July 8, 1863. During the siege the 21st was serving duty with heavy artillery. Their mission was to knock holes in the defenses of the fort at Port Hudson. However, during one shot this idea backfired. Sergeant Dooley, who was sighting the gun and noting the shots' effect, recalled:

> The immense shell—more like a big iron nail keg than a shot—went straight to the mark aimed at, and exploded just as it struck the hard packed face of the Confederate work. In fact it timed the explosion so well that the reaction was all one way; it hardly "fazed" the work, and all the pieces flew back to us. One big piece sailed high above our heads and struck in a hollow behind us. I only watched it till I saw it clear of us and

went on with my business, thinking, though, that we were a little too near the mark for comfort. Soon after we learned that the big piece had struck a man who was down in the hollow and crushed his skull.[1]

Odd Sense of Timing

Some people seem to have an odd sense of timing and because of this odd timing they have a knack for getting themselves in all sorts of trouble. It is not known whether Private James W. Hyatt of Company H, 118th Pennsylvania Volunteers, was one of these people, but at least once he nearly paid a dear price for his poor timing.

During the Mine Run Campaign in late November 1863 Private Hyatt indeed had a very close call. At about 2 a.m. on November 30, 1863, the 118th was ordered to a new position to ready themselves for an assault on the Confederate entrenchments the next morning. Before leaving for their new position, the men were ordered to strip themselves of any unnecessary articles including knapsacks. These were placed on a pile and a detachment of men was left behind to guard the personal effects. Private Hyatt apparently did not trust the guards and carried his knapsack. He was fortunate that the night was dark and he could violate the orders without being caught. In addition no fires or lights were permitted so Confederate troops would not detect the position change.

When the sun rose, the men prepared to make the assault. They were stationed on the edge of a pine woods with the rebel entrenchments only about five hundred yards in their front. Before the assault began, an artillery barrage opened upon the Confederate line. The rebels were quick to reply with their own artillery.[2] The men of the 118th crouched as low as they could to avoid the incoming shells. At this time Private Hyatt rose up and planted his knees on his knapsack and proceeded to tighten the blanket straps. While doing so he began to speak about being valorous. "As he worked at his straps and proceeded with his little speech, a solid shot dashed into the ground some distance in front of him, passed underneath him and the knapsack and striking the root of a tree splintered it and sent up to the surface a piece which took the heel off his right shoe."[3]

The incident quickly put an end to his speech and raised him a foot or more into the air. Stretcher-bearers were summoned and took the private to the rear where he recovered from the shock. The following May Private Hyatt was captured during the Battle of the Wilderness. He was sent to the Andersonville Prison in Georgia where he eventually died on December 3, 1864.[4]

A Lucky Chaplain

During this same time period the chaplain of the 118th had a close call of his own. Chaplain William J. O'Neill was one of the men left behind to guard the knapsacks while the remainder of the 118th moved to their new position for an assault on the Confederate entrenchments at Mine Run. Chaplain O'Neill had just made a pot of coffee.

Chaplain William J. O'Neill's coffee cup was knocked out of his hand by an incoming artillery shell.

History of the Corn Exchange Regiment

While he was sipping some of the warm brew from a tin cup, a Confederate shell flew into the camp and struck a nearby tree. When the shell burst, one of its fragments struck the tin cup and knocked it out of Chaplain O'Neill's hand. The chaplain wasn't hurt but his coffee was certainly ruined.[5]

Saved by the Good Book

Religion played an important part in the lives of many men during the Civil War. It was not unusual for a man to carry a Testament that could be read in times of great need. Private David Salmon of Company E, 93rd Pennsylvania Volunteers, was one of those men who could definitely say he was saved by the Good Book.

On May 5, 1862, the 93rd had arrived on the outskirts of Williamsburg, Virginia. They were part of the Union army's drive to Richmond called the Peninsula Campaign. As they neared the historic Virginia town, men exhausted from marching littered the roadside. In the distance the sound of cannon beckoned. Finally at two o'clock the regiment was ordered into a dense woods where the men were allowed to lie down for a rest. After about a half hour the time came for the men to rise and form a line of battle. They took position on the road leading into Williamsburg. Here a rebel battle line advanced to within sixty yards of the 93rd when the Pennsylvania men opened fire with a volley. The Confederate line was stunned and forced back. It had been the 93rd's first real taste of battle. The fight lasted until about six o'clock in the evening when the guns fell silent and the Union force owned its part of the field.[6]

It was during the first Confederate volley that Private Salmon had a close call with death but was saved by the word of God. As the Confederate volley tore into the Federal ranks, Private Salmon was hit in the right breast at the blouse pocket. Salmon was knocked to the ground by what normally would have been a fatal shot. Being in near lifeless condition he was picked up and quickly taken to the rear for medical attention. Upon examination there was no sign of blood where the minié ball had struck. Instead "a blue spot, the size of a man's hand marked the place where he was struck." Fortunately for Private Salmon the contents of the blouse pocket saved him from an early death. In the pocket he carried a New Testament, a memorandum book, and a small paper of sugar. It was the Testament that stopped the ball from penetrating his body. Years later he would write, "my life was saved by a testament given to me by my best girl before leaving Lock Haven."[7] Private Salmon kept the book as a souvenir and in his elderly years fondly recalled, "I still have the New Testament and can surely say, that the word of God is able to save not only the soul but the body as well."[8]

Almost Lost His Head

The phrase "timing is everything" fit the Civil War experience of Lieutenant Jacob Green very well. The thirty-nine-year-old Bavarian immigrant had only been in the army for one month when he found himself on the bank of Antietam Creek in one of the bloodiest battles of the war.

It was late in the afternoon. The 9th New Hampshire had just crossed the Rohrbach Bridge (Burnside Bridge) and was waiting for orders to move up the hill on the west bank of the creek. Lieutenant Green sat with his back against a tree trying to gain a few moments of rest before the movement. Suddenly a Confederate battery opened fire upon the position. The men of Company I quickly ran for cover as the shells tore through the trees throwing foliage and branches upon them. However, Lieutenant Green, comfortable where he sat, was content to stay in his position. Suddenly a second volley of shells came crashing into the trees. Again the lieutenant remained in his position, but this time he ducked down for cover. When the shelling was over, Lieutenant Green picked himself up from the ground. Looking back at the tree he had just recently been leaning against, he declared in his native Bavarian tongue, "Mein Gott, boys, see vere I haf been sitting!" As it turned out, his timing for ducking was perfect. Had he waited even seconds to lower his head, the lieutenant would have rested in peace under the tree for eternity. There, embedded in the tree at the spot where Lieutenant Green's head had been resting a short time earlier, was a round shot.[9]

The Keys to Survival

Many times soldiers were deceived by their wounds. Battles are chaotic in nature. The noise of guns and men screaming plus the blinding smoke play on a person's senses. One of the victims of this confusion was Lieutenant Isaac Plumb of the 61st New York Volunteers. His experience during the Battle of Gettysburg was certainly remarkable.

On July 2, 1863, the Wheatfield near the town of Gettysburg was the scene of some of the most horrific fighting of the war. During the action Lieutenant Plumb was hit by a minié ball and knocked down. In a natural reaction the lieutenant cupped his hands over the wound. Being hit in the chest he felt it would not be long before he would black out and his life's blood would slowly flow from his body. He had seen this before and knew that his chances of survival were low. Lieutenant Plumb waited for death to collect his soul while the fury of battle still raged around him. But after several minutes Lieutenant Plumb was still conscious. It was then that he decided to examine his wound. Slowly lifting his hands he noticed they were clean of blood and there was no blood on his blouse. It was then he realized that he felt only a little pain; certainly not the pain of a minié ball blowing open a hole in his chest. Finally, feeling he was not seriously hurt, Lieutenant Plumb stood up. By this time the men of the 61st were leaving the field and the lieutenant took his place back in the line.

That night Lieutenant Plumb prepared to get some much-needed sleep. While unbuckling his sword belt he noticed a strange formation in his vest pocket. It was in this pocket that he had kept a ring full of keys. Examining the keys he noticed a ball embedded in them. Luckily for Lieutenant Plumb when he was hit, the minié ball first struck his belt plate and glanced off hitting him in the vest pocket and the keys.[10]

As lucky as Lieutenant Plumb was that day in the Wheatfield at Gettysburg his luck would not last. At Cold Harbor on June 11, 1864, Lieutenant Plumb received another, but more severe, wound. This time there was nothing that would deflect the ball from its deadly journey, and on July 4 Lieutenant Plumb died of his injury.[11]

Rude Awakening

After the Civil War Second Lieutenant Randolph Shotwell of the 8th Virginia Infantry became a prominent journalist living in North Carolina.[12] However, it was only sheer luck that allowed him to survive one close call.

Lieutenant Randolph Shotwell had a rude wakeup call at Cold Harbor when an artillery shell tore the blanket he was holding.

The Papers of Randolph Abbott Shotwell

In his memoirs Lieutenant Shotwell describes a very rude morning wakeup call at Cold Harbor on Saturday, June 4, 1864. It was the day after the great charge that took the lives of over seven thousand Union men in less than an hour's time. On this day everything was quiet with the exception of shots being exchanged between pickets. With the lines less than half a mile apart and some places even closer, this firing was dangerous. The rifle pits occupied by Lieutenant Shotwell and the 8th Virginia were in a wooded area thick with young pines and cedar trees. The rifle pits were located about three hundred yards in advance of the main rebel entrenchments and were therefore in quite an exposed position to the Union lines. Of the experience Lieutenant Shotwell wrote, "Lieutenant [John] Gray and myself were shaking out a blanket at sunrise, each of us holding one end of it, when whiz-z-z! and a well-aimed shell from a small cannon that the Yankees had brought to the edge of the woods during the night, split the blanket between us, and killed a man several hundred yards to the rear. The breadth of a hair in the aim, or 'sighting' would have killed one or both of us, and saved the man coming up behind."[13] Lieutenant Shotwell's day, however, did not improve very much. Late in the afternoon he became separated from his command and was captured. The remainder of his Civil War career was spent at Fort Delaware, a Union prison on the Delaware River.[14]

Gordon's Rough Day at Antietam

Some of the most intense fighting of the Civil War occurred during the Battle of Antietam. During the morning hours the fighting raged back and forth, focusing much of its energy on a cornfield owned by a local farmer. By late morning the two armies had exhausted themselves on that portion of the field. A much-needed lull came over the land as round two was about to begin. The scene shifted to the right and the center of the Confederate line. Here Southerners positioned themselves in an old sunken farm road that was normally used as an avenue for more peaceful means, such as hauling grain to market. However, this September day would not be peaceful along its eroded bed.

Positioned in the lane was the 6th Alabama commanded by Colonel John B. Gordon. Not a military man, Gordon had training in law and was engaged in developing coal mines in Georgia when the war broke out.[15] Now, coal mining was far from his mind as he stood waiting anxiously for the expected assault. At this time the men were visited by General Robert E. Lee who used the lull in the action to survey his defenses. As Lee passed by the line, Gordon took the time to boost the morale of his men when he shouted to the commander, "These men are going to stay here, General, till the sun goes down or victory is won."[16] However, for Gordon it wasn't just an empty, dramatic boost. In his memoirs he wrote about his feelings of being killed in battle:

> My extraordinary escapes from wounds in all the previous battles had made a deep impression upon my comrades as well as upon my own mind. So many had fallen at my side, so often had balls and shells pierced and torn my clothing, grazing my body without drawing a drop of blood, that a sort of blind faith possessed my men that I was not to be killed in battle. This belief was evidenced by their constantly repeated expressions: "They can't hurt him." "He's as safe one place as another." He's got a charmed life.[17]

Soon the expected assault came. Colonel Gordon waited for the Union lines to reach within a few rods of the road when he ordered his men to fire. The Union line reeled at the blast and soon retreated. Several more attempts were made to break the center of the line but the stubborn Confederates held.

As the battle for the sunken lane intensified, Colonel Gordon's luck ran out when he was hit in the calf of his right leg. Soon another ball struck the same leg but higher up. Both balls only penetrated flesh, not hitting any bones, allowing Gordon to remain upright. Gordon persisted in walking the line encouraging his men and giving orders. A third ball struck his left arm "tearing asunder the tendons and mangling the flesh." At this point he was urged by his men to retire from the field, but he refused to leave them. A fourth ball tore into his shoulder. Looking to the right of the line he noticed the men beginning to waver. Remembering his pledge to the army's commander, Gordon began to move in that direction in an effort to solidify the position. By now the shock and loss of blood was taking its toll on his body. Suddenly a fifth ball hit him squarely in the face. Gordon fell unconscious to the ground. Now the danger wasn't from wounds but from the possibility of

Colonel John B. Gordon was saved from drowning in his own blood by a bullet hole in his hat.

MOLLUS-MASS Coll. at USAMHI

suffocating in his own blood. Oddly, when Gordon fell to the ground, he fell with his face in his hat. As he lay, blood trickled into the newly formed reservoir. It would not have taken long for the blood to cut off the oxygen supply. However, in an ironic piece of luck Gordon's life was saved by a sixth Yankee minié ball. This ball didn't strike flesh but sometime during the fighting had drilled a hole into his hat. It was this hole that served as a drain allowing the flow of blood to exit the hat and not starve the Confederate colonel from a vital breath of air.

After the battle at the Sunken Road Colonel Gordon was taken to a barn in the rear where he regained consciousness late that night.[18] John Gordon eventually recovered from his wounds and was promoted for his service to brigadier general then major general. He served for the remainder of the war, finally surrendering in April 1865 at Appomattox Court House. His postwar service included serving as a United States senator and governor of Georgia.[19]

Artillery for Supper

Food, let alone good food, was usually rare in either army during the Civil War. Therefore when soldiers were able to acquire a good meal they were certainly most delighted. John L. Parker in his *History of the Twenty-Second Massachusetts Infantry* related a story of what occurs when one of these special treats is mixed with an artillery bombardment:

> One day a member of Company A had gotten hold of some green apples, and started to make some sauce. He prepared his apples, and put them in a tin dish on a fire, and was so absorbed in his work, that he did not notice a shell coming over from the rebel battery with

its vicious "Where-is-he? Where-is-he?" which every old soldier well remembers. Sitting on his heels, alternately poking the fire and stirring the mess, he was all unconscious of danger, when the shell struck plump in his dish. With a veteran's instinct, he threw himself backwards flat on the ground just as the shell exploded, filling the air with fragments of iron, fire-brands, stewed apples and sacred soil. Our patriot gathered himself, and apparently with but a single thought, glared fiercely at the hole where his hopes had disappeared, and said, "There's that apple-sarse gone to hell!"[20]

Blanket Protection

At the Battle of Antietam on September 17, 1862, the 6th Wisconsin saw more than their fair share of the fight. During the morning phase of the battle the 6th was engaged in the horrific fighting in the Miller Cornfield. By late afternoon the men of the 6th were assigned to support a line of artillery batteries. The men could hear the fighting raging off to their far right as General Ambrose Burnside's IX Corps struggled to cross the Rohrbach Bridge. Suddenly, Confederate artillery opened upon their position. The men quickly scurried to

Major Rufus Dawes barely escaped death when a shell landed between him and Captain John Kellogg.

MOLLUS-MASS Coll. at USAMHI

find shelter from the incoming rounds. Major Rufus Dawes and Captain John Kellogg found safety on the ground. Major Dawes tells what happened next, "We lay as closely as possible to the ground. I was upon the same oil-cloth with Captain John A. Kellogg, when a large fragment of shell passed into the ground between us, cutting a great hole in the oil-cloth, and covering us with dirt. It was a mystery how this could be and neither of us be struck."[21]

Good Advice

Sergeant John W. Stuart of Company G, 148th Pennsylvania Volunteers, had an interesting account of dumb luck. Stuart was only seventeen years old when he enlisted in the army. The first two years of his enlistment passed without incident as he survived the various battles in which the 148th was engaged. However, his luck seemed to have run out on May 10, 1864, at the Po River. During the engagement Sergeant Stuart was hit by a minié ball passing through his cartridge box. Upon recovering his breath he felt around his back to find where the ball had exited his body. To his amazement there was no wound. In fact he soon realized that the ball had not penetrated his abdomen. His life had been saved by his cartridge box. This in itself was a piece of luck since he strayed from the norm by carrying the box in his front instead of to the side like most soldiers did. For this bit of fortune Sergeant Stuart owed Corporal George Duffy. Corporal Duffy was standing beside Stuart during the action and suggested that Stuart wear his cartridge box in front of him that it might stop a bullet. The suggestion worked. Luckily for Stuart the cartridge could not have been full or else his entire ration of ammunition could have exploded, causing a much greater injury than the single minié ball would have.[22]

Corporal George Duffy was a special individual in the regiment. Captain James J. Patterson of Company G wrote that "Corporal Duffy was an ideal soldier, brave, cool and trustworthy; as a scout reliable; on post vigilant, quick to discover and interpret any movement of the enemy; an unerring shot, cheerful under the performance of every duty, honorable in all his ways and a gentleman in his instincts."[23] Unfortunately for Duffy he was shot through both legs two days later at Spotsylvania. When stretcher-bearers arrived, he insisted they look after another soldier lying nearby and then come back for him. However, the battle lines shifted and when the stretcher-bearers returned, Duffy was outside the Union position. The next morning the regiment advanced but it was too late. Corporal Duffy was already dead.[24]

Sergeant Stuart was sent to Washington where he recovered from his wound, which even though slight was very painful. He remained in the hospital for three months and then returned to the 148th. In February he was promoted to second lieutenant, the youngest officer of the regiment. He went on to serve as the regimental quartermaster until the close of the war.[25] In June 1865 the 148th was finally mustered out of the service and Lieutenant Stuart returned home to central Pennsylvania.[26]

Pencils Aren't Just for Writing

James Beaver was indeed a veteran when he was mustered out of the service in December 1864. As colonel of the 148th Pennsylvania he saw service at the battles at Chancellorsville, Gettysburg, the Wilderness, Spotsylvania, and Petersburg, just to name a few. In the course of these battles he was wounded several times: in the right hip, the left side, and the right thigh, which caused his right leg to be amputated. However, it was his first wound in which he denied fate.[27]

The 148th was a fairly new regiment to the Union Army of the Potomac in the spring of 1862. It had just been mustered into service in September and joined the main army in late December, just missing the Battle of Fredericksburg by several days.[28]

The first test of the Pennsylvania men was the Battle of Chancellorsville in May 1863. Here the 148th saw limited action with only Companies C, D, G, and H being involved. During this engagement the four companies of the 148th had entered the thick underbrush of the Wilderness that surrounded the Chancellor Mansion. The Union line was receiving a withering fire forcing Colonel Beaver to order the men to lie down. At this time Beaver was anxious to communicate with Brigade Commander General John Curtis Caldwell. Just as he drew the attention of his commander, Beaver was hit by a rebel minié ball. In the regimental history of the 148th, Colonel Beaver tells what happened next:

> . . . I fell violently upon my face, my sword flying from my hand and, when I turned upon my back, found a hole in my clothing just beneath the two rows of buttons. Without stopping to consider the matter, I inferred that a ball had entered there and that my military service was ended. A couple of the boys who had seen me fall ran up to me and one of them, taking off his blanket was preparing to roll me in it, so as to take me away, but I said to them that it would be time enough to bury the dead after the fight was over and that they had better leave me alone.

The men did not heed their colonel's advice and deemed it best to get him out of the range of rebel guns. They dragged their commander along the ground until coming across some stretcher-bearers who took him to the hospital. Once at the hospital Beaver was laid on a table where Dr. George L. Potter examined the wound. Colonel Beaver recalled:

> Lying upon my back, looking into his face [Potter's], I could see the deep concern which he manifested. After opening my clothing and examining the wound,

Colonel James Beaver was saved from a mortal wound by a pencil.

The Story of Our Regiment: A History of the 148th Pennsylvania Volunteers

however, and putting his little fingers into the apertures of the wound—there being two of them—I noticed, before he said a word, a great change in his face followed by, "Ah, Beaver, that's all right." The ball had struck me in the side . . . and had evidently struck a gutta percha lead pencil. . . . This had been shattered into a half dozen or more pieces and had evidently turned the course of the ball, so that it went through only the fleshy part of the abdomen and did not enter the abdominal cavity.

Colonel Beaver was able to return to his home in Bellefonte, Pennsylvania. He soon recovered and rejoined the army in the middle of July.[29] After the war Colonel Beaver went on to become governor of Pennsylvania and later president of the Pennsylvania State University.

Chapter Eight

Civil War Medicine

A Probing Wound

Pickett's Charge during the third day at Gettysburg was climactic. The Confederate assault was thrown back and victory secured for the Union. However, victory came at a price. Major General Winfield Scott Hancock, commander of the Union II Corps and one of the ablest commanders of the army, was wounded.

Hit in the groin during the charge, Hancock refused to leave the field until the battle was over. Instead, he was examined by Medical Director Alexander Dougherty. Arriving about fifteen minutes after the general was wounded, Dougherty was able to remove "several pieces of wood, and a wrought-iron ten penny nail bent double, which had entered the leg near the groin."[1]

No ball was discovered. The wood and nail were from Hancock's own saddle. Evidently the ball had struck the saddle tree and forced the wood splinters and nail into Hancock's groin.

General Hancock telegraphed his wife, Almira, informing her, "I am severely wounded, not mortally. Join me at once in Philadelphia."[2]

On July 6 General Hancock arrived in Philadelphia to be joined by his wife.[3] While in Philadelphia there was no sign that the healing process had begun. In fact, Hancock experienced increased discomfort at this time.[4] Several attempts were made to examine the wound in order to ascertain whether a ball or other foreign object was still lodged in the groin. However, nothing could be found. After each failure Hancock sank deeper in despair at the thought that the wound might be fatal.[5]

After some time Hancock's doctors decided he should be moved out of the city to his father's home in Norristown, Pennsylvania. On the day of the move a squad of city firemen arrived at the hotel La Piere where Hancock convalesced while staying in Philadelphia. The men carefully moved the "worn and shattered" general to the Philadelphia Depot. Upon arriving in Norristown a detachment of the Invalid Guards met Hancock and carried him through the streets of the town to his father's home.[6]

As the month of August wore on, several more doctors made the attempt at examining the groin wound without success. However, most of the physicians still agreed that there was a foreign object, possibly a minié ball that kept the wound from healing.

By late August the general had all but given up hope. At this time he was paid a visit by Dr. Louis Read, medical director of the Pennsylvania Reserves. Doctor Read found Hancock ". . . much disheartened. He had grown thin, and looked pale and emaciated." Hancock welcomed his visitor and expressed his growing despair at the continual, unsuccessful examinations and that he felt the wound was going to be fatal. When Dr. Read prepared to leave the meeting,

Hancock bid him goodbye and remarked that they might never meet again. Then Hancock inquired if the surgeon wouldn't make an attempt to probe the wound himself. Dr. Read thought for a moment and then agreed. Dr. Read noted that all the examinations occurred while Hancock was on his back and his leg at a right angle to the body. Dr. Read rationalized that if Hancock was wounded while astride his horse it would make sense to probe the wound with the general seated in the same fashion. At this point the general was willing to try almost anything and took little convincing at the different approach.

Hancock was helped up on the dining room table and positioned on a chair. The doctor then began probing the wound. Carefully he stuck the probe into the wounded leg. The flesh was sore from the previous probings, making the process slow and agonizing for the sick general. But this was possibly his last chance for survival, and the discomfort had to be endured. Finally after being inserted eight inches, the probe struck a minié ball that had imbedded itself in the bone.

Major General Winfield Scott Hancock suffered for weeks when surgeons failed to locate the minié ball lodged in his groin.

MOLLUS-MASS Coll. at USAMHI

The next day, August 22, Dr. Read performed surgery on the general. The ball that caused so much pain was finally removed. Now after seven weeks of suffering, General Hancock was relieved of his source of pain and could begin the healing process.[7]

Eventually Hancock was able to return to service in the Army of the Potomac. However, the wound he acquired at Gettysburg that festered for weeks after remained a burden throughout the rest of the war.[8]

The Look of Death

The scene of a Civil War battlefield after the fighting ceased was horrific. In numerous personal accounts soldiers and civilians alike have described the terrible sights. Captain Richard Musgrove of the 12th New Hampshire Volunteers described what he saw while exploring a portion of the Gettysburg battlefield:

> Evidences of the fearful strife that had taken place were on every hand—broken caissons, disabled guns and gun carriages, small arms in profusion, knapsacks and canteens were lying about, dead horses not yet buried and wounded horses looking with almost human faces at one for relief . . . The dead lay here so thick that it was with difficulty that we could walk without stepping on the lifeless forms. The features of all had turned black and maggots were crawling in and out of the gaping wounds.[9]

One odd recollection of the bodies that lay on the field of Gettysburg is mentioned by Reverend J. D. Bloodgood in his *Personal Reminiscences of the War.* While walking over the battlefield Reverend Bloodgood was struck by the differences in the appearance of the dead men from both armies. He

Captain Richard Musgrove witnessed the devastation left on the battlefield at Gettysburg.

Autobiography of Capt. Richard Musgrove

said, "The rebel dead retained nearly their natural appearance, while our dead [Union soldiers] had almost invariably turned a very dark purple in the face."[10] The reverend did not offer a reason for such a difference in complexions. Was it diet? Generally Union troops were better fed than their Southern counterparts. Or was it weather? Southern men were more adapted to the heat of the sun. Having been exposed to the sun's direct rays while lying on the battlefield they were possibly not affected like their Northern brothers who had lived in a cooler climate. This is just another mystery that was buried with the dead during one of the war's greatest battles.

A Hair-raising Incident

One of the most bizarre incidents of the Civil War actually occurred after the war. Corporal Henry Matthews of Company H, 48th Pennsylvania Volunteers, was wounded during the battle of Cold Harbor on June 3, 1864. The ball entered the back of his head and lodged behind the forehead. Surgery was performed and the ball removed. During the operation a portion of the brain was taken out "weighing about an ounce and a half and as large as an egg . . ."

Corporal Matthews recovered from his wound and was released from the hospital. He was given the bullet, which should have killed him, as a souvenir. It was flattened from impact and shaped somewhat like a "miniature clam shell." However, the doctor did not take the time to clean the ball. Therefore, when Corporal Matthews received his "souvenir," part of the brain matter and scalp still adhered to it.

For whatever reason Matthews also neglected to clean the ball and simply kept it as it was given him. Occasionally he would look at the ball that nearly killed him. As time passed by he noticed something peculiar about his war relic. The hairs that remained in the scalp were growing. In fact other hairs had emerged and grown until a "thick black bunch appeared at the back end of the bullet." Even after cutting the hairs they continued to grow at the astonishment of the owner.

After several years Corporal Matthews traveled to Philadelphia to look up Dr. W. R. D. Blackwood, the surgeon who removed the bullet from Matthew's forehead. Dr. Blackwood examined the hairy bullet and proceeded to cut off about an inch of hair and measured the remainder. He then sealed the bullet in a box. After about a year the box was opened by Dr. Blackwood and the hair measured again. To his astonishment the hair had grown about an inch while sealed inside the box.

Upon this discovery Dr. Blackwood explained, "The fact is beyond dispute. Apparently without nutrition, upon the dried up particle of scalp and brain, this hair had been and is now growing as surely if not so luxuriantly as it grew upon Matthews' head when he was shot. I recollect the wound, the operation, and the presentation of the relic to the injured man after his remarkable recovery. It seems to me to settle beyond doubt that hair can and does grow upon dead bodies. . . ."[11]

Coughing Bullets

Captain Connally Litchfield of Company D, 1st Virginia Cavalry, had a knack for being wounded in battle. He was hit a total of six times during his Civil War career. However, Captain Litchfield was not a quitter. Instead he always went back for more and was at Appomattox Court House when General Robert E. Lee surrendered the Confederate Army of Northern Virginia. Even then he was not content to give up and slipped through the Union lines with Major General Thomas Rosser.

One of Captain Litchfield's closest calls with death was the last time he was wounded. This one proved to be quite amazing. It was at the Battle of Winchester, Virginia, on September 19, 1864, when he received a pistol shot to the face. The ball penetrated just under his left eye. The wound was probed by a surgeon, but the ball was not found. Captain Litchfield patiently waited until the wound healed and then returned to active duty with the ball still lodged in his face.[12]

After the war Captain Litchfield settled down to civilian life in Abingdon, Virginia. However, things were not back to normal. He still carried the pistol ball in his cheek and was reminded of its presence by a constant barrage of pain. In addition he had to live with a discharge of pus and water from his left eye, causing the eventual loss of sight in that eye.

When the pain became too great to bear, Captain Litchfield took morphine. The pain would be eased but the side effect to the morphine was a bout of nausea. For Captain Litchfield there was no way he could win. For over thirty years he was forced to bear the pain and misery of his old war wound. But then, ironically, it was the nausea that eventually eased Litchfield's suffering.

In July 1897 Litchfield suffered unbearable pain in his cheek. It was so bad that he turned to the morphine to dull the pain knowing full well he would be sick from the medicine. Like clockwork the usual attack of nausea overcame the captain after he took the painkiller. However, this particular bout of vomiting was more violent than normal, and Captain Litchfield felt something hard drop into his mouth which was then expelled into the pan he was using. To his amazement in the pan lay the pistol ball that had caused so much anguish and pain for the last thirty-four years.[13]

How to Be Relieved from Duty

"If I was to turn back now, many would say I was a coward. I would rather be shot at once than to have such a stigma rest on me," David Beem wrote to his wife early in the war.[14] These are words that are reflected in many letters written by soldiers on both sides of the Civil War. However, there were also men who did their best to shirk duty whether it be guard duty or battle.

John D. Billings wrote in his book *Hardtack and Coffee* of a man who faked rheumatism in order to be discharged. Billings writes: "He responded daily to sick call, pitifully warped out of shape, was prescribed for, but all to no avail. One leg was drawn up so that, apparently, he could not use it, and groans indicative of excruciating agony escaped him at studied intervals and on suitable occasions."

For six weeks the ruse went on until finally the surgeon recommended the "ailing" man be discharged. Delighted at his accomplishment the soldier began to celebrate with whiskey. Soon the liquor took a hold of the man's senses and he became drunk. At this point he was not able to keep up the ruse and it was quickly discovered that he was in full control of both legs. The discharge was revoked and the man was made to pay for his deception for months afterward.[15]

Other soldiers went to more serious methods to obtain a discharge. Self-mutilation by shooting off a toe was one way of getting a quick ride home.[16]

A less violent method helped several men to be placed on sick call instead of performing other duties. The following was recorded by Dr. Albert Gaillard Hart in his memoirs, *The Surgeon and the Hospital in the Civil War.* For several consecutive mornings men reported to sick call complaining of backaches, headaches, and a very heavily coated tongue. Upon investigating, Dr. Hart did indeed find that their tongues were heavily coated. Fearing they were coming down with a fever, the doctor immediately excused the men from duty. However, after being faked out several times, the surgeon caught on that it was all a hoax. Later he was informed that the men would chew on rose leaves that could be found liberally around the camp. Chewing on the leaves would leave a residue on their tongues, deceiving the surgeon into thinking that they were coming down with a fever.

Another ingenious method for being relieved from duty was perpetrated in a New York regiment during the winter of 1861. Once again soldiers showed up at sick call with coated tongues. The mystery was solved when the surgeon, upon investigation, found a druggist among the enlisted men. In the good name of capitalism the druggist was supplying a white mixture for a small fee to anyone needing time off from duty.[17]

Left for Dead

When studying Civil War battles and reading battle reports it is very often hard to believe that anyone could walk away from a battle without being wounded. But many men did just that. On the other hand, there are the men who seemed to have attracted minié balls and received more than their fair share of wounds. Private Edward P. Rockwood of Company H, 25th Massachusetts, was one such soldier. Enlisting on September 13, 1861, he was able to maneuver himself through the next several years of war unscathed. However, after re-enlisting in January 1864 his luck turned for the worse.[18]

In early June the 25th participated in the battle of Cold Harbor, Virginia. During the battle the order came to charge the Confederate works. The 25th charged ". . . gallantly for some distance through the most galling fire, until within a few yards of their [Confederate] entrenchment, when they were met by a storm of bullets, shot, and shell that no human power could withstand."[19]

During the charge Private Rockwood received the first of several wounds. A minié ball struck him in the chin, fracturing the bone and tearing out several teeth. Another hit his right shoulder and a third passed through his abdomen. When the private fell to the ground, several men grabbed him and dragged him to a hole. However, Private Rockwood's ordeal was not over. His head and body were now protected but not his legs and feet. While lying in the hole, another Confederate ball hit him in the calf of his leg, still another struck his shin. A third ball cut through the top of his instep while the fourth almost severed a toe. A Confederate surgeon completed the amputation.[20]

That night Confederates combed the field for any survivors of the assault. Once they came upon Private Rockwood they gave him up for dead, figuring a surgeon's attention would be pointless. However, several of his captured comrades insisted on helping him. Placing the wounded man in a blanket they carried him from the field. Private Rockwood was wounded a total of seven times that day at Cold Harbor.[21] He was eventually sent to a rebel prison where he was exchanged on November, 26, 1864, and discharged for wounds on July 7, 1865.[22]

Chapter Nine

Tempting Fate

To Be Buried in Such a Beautiful Spot

Major General Patrick Cleburne looked upon St. John's Episcopal Church near Ashwood, Tennessee, with interest.[1] The church lay on his route as he led his division toward Nashville. Cleburne's division was part of the Army of Tennessee, which had begun an offensive in the fall of 1864 designed to detract Major General William Sherman's Union army away from its infamous March to the Sea.

Cleburne was one of the South's shining stars. Ironically, he wasn't Southern-born but had adopted the cause of the South after emigrating from Ireland years before. Having been tested in many of the major battles of the western theater, Cleburne earned a reputation for being a quality commander. He had also earned a reputation for being outspoken. It was Cleburne who first publicly suggested that slaves be enlisted in the Confederate army—a suggestion that won him much scorn across the South.[2]

At this time the Southern cause was in doubt. In the East the Army of Northern Virginia was besieged in the cities of Richmond and Petersburg. The Southern cause wasn't faring any better in the West. Major General William T. Sherman had left the city of Atlanta in ruins and was cutting a huge swath of destruction across Georgia during his March to the Sea.

In Ashwood, Cleburne admired St. John's Church and its adjacent cemetery. Turning to his aide, Captain C. H. Hill, he commented, "it would not be hard to die if one could be buried in such a beautiful spot."[3]

Several days later on November 30 the Army of Tennessee arrived at the town of Franklin. Entrenched outside the town was the Union Army of Ohio commanded by Major General John Schofield. For the Confederates, Nashville was to be a brief stop as they crushed the Union force in the city. It was late in the day when the rebel army formed into battle lines. After deploying his troops, Cleburne rode to General John Bell Hood, commander of the Army of Tennessee, and stated, "General, I am ready, and have more hope in the final success of our cause than I have had at any time since the first gun was fired." To this Hood replied, "God grant it!"[4]

Around 4 p.m. the order was given to move forward. Cleburne followed his division into the storm of the battle. The Confederate assault pushed back the first line of Union defenders. Suddenly Cleburne's mount

Major General Patrick Cleburne was so struck by the beauty of St. John's Episcopal Church that he told an aide, "it would not be hard to die if one could be buried in such a beautiful spot."

MOLLUS-MASS Coll. at USAMHI

was killed only eighty yards from the main line of Federal defenses. Another mount was quickly offered to the general. While he was mounting the new horse, it too was killed. Cleburne proceeded forward on foot. However, his turn to die came when a minié ball pierced his breast just below the heart.[5]

The next day Cleburne's body was discovered about sixty yards from the Federal works. Someone had taken the liberty of relieving the corpse of its boots, watch, and sword belt.[6] On December 2 the body of Patrick Cleburne was moved to the Rose Hill Cemetery at Columbia, Tennessee, and buried. However, it was soon discovered that the burial site was unsatisfactory since the grave was close to the graves of several Union soldiers. Cleburne's body, along with those of several other Confederates that had been killed at Franklin, were disinterred. A suitable resting place was found several miles away at St. John's Episcopal Church at Ashwood.[7] It was the same church that had caused Cleburne to comment that "it would not be hard to die if one could be buried in such a beautiful spot."[8]

To Die in Old Pennsylvania

In June 1863 the Confederate Army of Northern Virginia was flush with victory, having soundly defeated the Union Army of the Potomac at the Battle of Chancellorsville. In June the Confederate army launched its greatest invasion of the North. Southern troops crossed the Potomac River, marched through Maryland, and stepped into Pennsylvania.

The Union Army of the Potomac was obliged to follow. For the Northern troops this was a different campaign. They were no longer invading a hostile territory. The luxury of defeat and then retreat back to Washington didn't exist. This time they were marching to defend their families and homes. However, the mood in the ranks of the Northern soldiers was not somber as might be expected. Instead, it was upbeat. Amos Judson in his *History of the Eighty-Third Pennsylvania* states, "During the whole march the spirits of the men of the Eighty-Third had increased in confidence as they neared the boundaries of Pennsylvania, and when they found that they were about to enter the threshold of their native State and fight upon her soil, their enthusiasm knew no bounds."[9]

The excitement of the Union soldiers was soon to grow when on July 1 the two armies finally met on the fields around the southern Pennsylvania town of Gettysburg. It was during this battle that the Northern troops could finally show their mettle. They had come home to fight and would not be denied victory.

For Colonel Strong Vincent the excitement was contagious as he heard of the fighting taking place at Gettysburg. His brigade was positioned outside Hanover, Pennsylvania, when word was received of the battle. As brigade commander, Vincent ordered the drum corps and color guard of the 83rd Pennsylvania to the front. Stirred by feelings of patriotism he ordered the flags to be unfurled. Then taking off his hat, he said, "What death more glorious can any man desire than to die on the soil of old Pennsylvania fighting for that flag."[10]

Colonel Strong Vincent was a soldier on the rise in the Army of the Potomac. Born in Erie, Pennsylvania, he had graduated from Harvard and practiced law before the war. When President Abraham Lincoln asked for troops to put down the rebellion, Colonel Vincent was one of the first to enlist. He originally mustered into a three-month regiment. After that term of service ended he reenlisted in the 83rd Pennsylvania

Volunteers as a lieutenant colonel. During the Peninsula Campaign he was promoted to full colonel of the regiment. The next May, Colonel Vincent again was promoted, this time to brigade commander after the Battle of Chancellorsville.[11]

As Vincent's brigade neared Gettysburg they were ordered to the front of Little Round Top on the left flank of the Union line. It was the second day of the battle and a sense of urgency was in the air. Confederate forces were pressing the Union left flank and there was no time to waste. Colonel Vincent no more than moved his brigade in position at the base of the hill when the rebel battle lines began their assault. Judson states in his *History of the Eighty-Third Pennsylvania,* ". . . a loud, fierce, distant yell was heard, as if pandemonium had broken loose and joined in the chorus of one grand, universal war whoop. On looking to the left and front, we saw Hood's [General John Bell Hood] whole division, of Longstreet's [General James Longstreet] corps, over a quarter of a mile off, charging in three lines on a double-quick, and, with bayonets fixed, coming down upon us." Seeing that he was easily outnumbered, Colonel Vincent immediately called for reinforcements. He then sent his horse to the rear and proceeded to mount a large rock in order to have a better view of the battle. Little Round Top was vital to the Union cause; if the Confederates secured the rocky hill they would have command of the battlefield. The first charge of the rebel line was met with a sheet of fire from the Union rifles. The rebels were driven back only to re-form and advance again. The fighting was becoming desperate as the Southern force nearly broke through, but the Union line held. Again the Confederate line fell back, only to re-form. A third assault was made. In the thick of the struggle Colonel Vincent did

When Colonel Strong Vincent entered Pennsylvania during the Gettysburg Campaign he was reported as saying, "what death more glorious can any man desire than to die on the soil of old Pennsylvania fighting for that flag."

MOLLUS-MASS Coll. at USAMHI

his best to urge his men to repel the rebel force. During the third charge Colonel Vincent jumped off the rock and was rallying his men to fight when he was hit. The ball entered his left groin and lodged in the right groin area.

In the midst of the fighting, Colonel Vincent was carried from the field and taken to the farmhouse of William Bushman. After being examined by a surgeon it was determined that nothing could be done. Oddly, at this time, Colonel Vincent experienced little pain and did not know that death was on the horizon. He began to arrange for passage home to Erie, Pennsylvania, when he was finally informed by the surgeon that he could not be moved. Becoming aware of his mortal condition, Colonel Vincent resigned himself to the fact of his impending death and requested his wife be summoned from home. As the days passed, Colonel Vincent weakened and by the 6th of July he could hardly speak. On the 7th it had become evident that his last fight was about over, and in an effort to speak the Lord's Prayer, Colonel Vincent passed into eternity. Unfortunately, due to an administrative mixup his wife was unable to be by his side. Hearing of the valor Colonel Vincent displayed on the field of Gettysburg, Army of the Potomac commander, Major General George Gordon Meade awarded Colonel Vincent with a general's star, promoting him to brigadier general.[12]

The Bullet Is Not Moulded

"I have come to feel that the bullet is not moulded which is to kill me," declared Lieutenant Colonel George Arrowsmith of the 157th New York Volunteers. It was July 1, 1863, and events were moving rapidly that would challenge Arrowsmith's statement.[13]

Lieutenant Colonel Arrowsmith was an educated man who graduated from New York's Madison University in 1859.[14] He thought that law was his future, but the outbreak of war put those thoughts on hold when he joined the 26th New York and became the captain of Company D. His service in the 26th was also short-lived when he became assistant adjutant general to Brigadier General Zealous B. Tower.[15] General Tower looked fondly upon the young soldier and in later years remarked, "It is my recollection that Captain Arrowsmith . . . never yielded to overwork of any kind, and was never absent for a day from his post of duty, but was actively efficient unto the end, and on every battle field he evinced the cool gallantry to which I have already given my testimony."[16] On August 23, 1862, Arrowsmith was named lieutenant colonel of the 157th New York and from then on would be associated with the fortunes of that regiment.[17]

During the morning of July 1 the men of the 157th marched toward the southern Pennsylvania town of Gettysburg. In the distance the sound of artillery fire could be heard. Colonel Arrowsmith had been ill and was not fully recovered as the regiment marched north. By his side rode the regimental surgeon Dr. H. C. Hendrick. Hearing the artillery fire, Arrowsmith turned to Hendrick and remarked, "There will be warm work today, Doctor." Hendrick, concerned about Arrowsmith's health, replied, "You must not go into the fight, Colonel; you are not strong enough." As the conversation went on, Arrowsmith spoke about the anxiety of going into battle for the first time. But he was a veteran and stated, "I have gotten over all that." It was then that he made his bold statement: " I have come to feel that the bullet is not moulded which is to kill me."

The 157th reached Gettysburg around noon on July 1 and proceeded north of the town to a position where the Mummasburg, Carlisle, and Harrisburg Roads joined. By this time in the day the battle had been raging for hours.

It wasn't long until shells began flying in the direction of the 157th. Several fell amongst the regiment, causing Arrowsmith and the other officers to dismount from their restless horses and direct the regiment on foot. Directly in front of the 157th the First Ohio Battery was positioned. Soon an artillery duel between the 1st Ohio and Page's Confederate battery drew special interest from the New Yorkers. It was during this exchange that a shot from one of the Ohio cannons lodged in the muzzle of a Confederate gun, effectively spiking the weapon.[18]

Before long the men of the 157th had to direct their attention elsewhere as a Confederate assault formed. The New Yorkers were thrust forward to reinforce Colonel Wladimir Krzyzanowski's brigade. The regiment approached within fifty yards of the Southern line when they were hit with volleys of musket fire on the front and right flanks by the 44th and 4th Georgia regiments. The 157th reeled at the blast when suddenly on their left flank the 21st Georgia, which had been concealed from view by lying in a lane, rose up and delivered a devastating volley.[19] Captain William Saxton described the scene, stating that "the men fell like daisies before the mower's scythe."[20]

Colonel Arrowsmith was directing the regiment on the right of the line to the rear of Company C. Not long after the 157th became engaged with the Georgia regiments, Arrowsmith was struck in the forehead by a rifle ball. As the fighting became more intense, the Southern line began to form a semi-circle around the 157th. Observing the dire situation that his regiment could be captured in whole, Colonel Philip Brown ordered his men to retreat. Unfortunately for Colonel Arrowsmith there was no time to help him from the field and he died soon after the retreat.[21] The day was disastrous for the rest of the 157th. When roll call was finally called, a total of 193 men were killed or wounded while 114 were missing. Of the 409 men engaged in the battle 75 percent became casualties.[22]

Almost Too Self-Assured

Lieutenant John Anderson in his *History of the 57th Regiment of Massachusetts Volunteers* described what happened to soldiers who had become too self-assured of their own safety.

On June 3, 1864, one of the dramatic events of the war took place at Cold Harbor, Virginia, when Lieutenant General Ulysses S. Grant ordered a massive assault against the Confederate entrenchments designed to literally smash through the rebel line. It would turn out to be one of the worst days of the war for the Northern cause. Over seven thousand Union men would be killed in less than an hour's time with the rebel works still intact.

It was during the morning hours that Lieutenant Anderson witnessed an incident that could easily be said to be an act of foolishness. At this time the 57th was supporting an artillery battery that was fighting a duel with a rebel battery posted in a wooded area about half a mile from the Union lines. During the incident one young man from the 57th desired a better view of the action and so seated himself upon a rotten tree stump. In the meantime the remainder of the men in the vicinity were lying on the ground in an effort to shelter themselves from the incoming artillery rounds. Several times the young man on the stump was cautioned about his dangerous position, but to no avail. Instead he boasted that "the shot had not been made that could hit him." Just at that moment a solid shot hit the stump, smashing it to pieces. The boastful young man suddenly found himself on the ground in a heap.[23]

Notes

Chapter One
Animal Curiosities

Sallie's Premonition

1. John D. Lippy, Jr., *The War Dog* (Harrisburg, Pa.: The Telegraph Press, 1962), 19.
2. *The Bivouac* (Boston: Bivouac Publishing Co., 1885), III, 18.
3. Lippy, *War Dog*, 34–36.
4. Ibid., 25.
5. Ibid., 38.

The Hogs of Gettysburg

6. Jay Jorgensen, *The Wheatfield at Gettysburg: A Walking Tour* (Gettysburg: Thomas Publications, 2002), 8.
7. Survivors Association of the 118th (Corn Exchange) Regt. P. V., *History of the Corn Exchange Regiment 118th Pennsylvania Volunteers* (Philadelphia: J. L. Smith, 1888), 711.
8. Ibid., 250.
9. Ibid., 711.
10. Richard W. Musgrove, *Autobiography of Capt. Richard W. Musgrove* (Mary D. Musgrove, 1921), 94–96.

By the Crow of a Rooster

11. Rev. William A. Keesy, *War as Viewed from the Ranks* (Norwalk, Ohio: The Experiment and News Co.), 222–223.
12. James Russell Soley, *The Navy in the Civil War: The Blockade and the Cruisers* (New York: Charles Scribner's Sons, 1883), 157.
13. Keesy, *War as Viewed from the Ranks*, 223.

Rats, Rats, and More Rats

14. James F. Robertson Jr., *Soldiers Blue and Gray* (Columbia: University of South Carolina, 1988), 199.

15. Henry Steele Commager, *The Blue and the Gray*, reprint (New York: The Fairfax Press, 1982), 699–700.

16. Ibid., 703.

17. W. A. Wash, *Camp, Field, and Prison Life* (Saint Louis: Southwestern Book and Publishing Co., 1870), 259–260.

Hospital Rats

18. Phoebe Yates Pember, *A Southern Woman's Story: Life in Confederate Richmond*, Bell Irvin Wiley ed. (Wilmington, N.C.: Broadfoot Publishing, 1991), 85–86.

Bad Water

19. St. Clair Mulholland, *The Story of the 116th Regiment Pennsylvania Volunteers in the War of the Rebellion* (Philadelphia: F. McManus, Jr. & Co., 1903), 114–115.

Pork for Dinner

20. W. H. Lee, "Johnnie and Yank Divide the Hog," *Confederate Veteran* (July 1909), 342.

Howling for His Master

21. Harry W. Pfanz, *Gettysburg, The Second Day* (Chapel Hill: The University of North Carolina Press, 1987), 321.

22. J. W. Muffly, *The Story of Our Regiment: A History of the 148th Pennsylvania Volunteers* (Des Moines: Kenyon Printing & Mfg. Co., 1904), 173.

23. Pfanz, *Gettysburg, The Second Day*, 434.

24. Muffly, *History of the 148th*, 172.

25. Ibid., 923.

26. Ibid., 173.

27. "Gettysburg Ghosts: Still Hearing the Guns," *Blue & Gray* (Fall 1997), 60.

28. Gerard A. Patterson, *Debris of Battle: The Wounded of Gettysburg* (Mechanicsburg: Stackpole Books, 1997), 143, 200.

29. *Blue & Gray*, 60.

Lice Racing

30. John D. Billings, *Hardtack and Coffee or The Unwritten Story of Army Life* (Gettysburg: Civil War Times Illustrated, 1974), 80.

31. Bell Irvin Wiley, *The Life of Johnny Reb: The Common Soldier of the Confederacy* (Indianapolis: The Bobbs-Merrill Company, 1943), 37–39.

32. B. A. Botkin, ed., *A Civil War Treasury of Tales, Legends, and Folklore* (New York: Promontory Press, 1960), 73.

Animal Graffiti

33. W. C. King and W. P. Derby, comps., *Camp-Fire Sketches and Battle-Field Echoes* (Springfield, Mass.: King, Richardson & Co., 1888), 387.

Chapter Two
Predictions

A Substitute for Death

1. Survivors Association, *History of the Corn Exchange Regiment*, 734.

2. Ibid., 672.

3. Ibid., 395.

4. Ibid., 672.

5. Ibid., 396–397.

6. Ibid., 399.

7. John Michael Priest, *Nowhere to Run: The Wilderness, May 4th & 5th, 1864* (Shippensburg: White Mane Publishing, 1995), 8.

8. William B. Styple, ed., *With A Flash of His Sword: The Writings of Major Holman S. Melcher 20th Maine Infantry* (Kearny, N.J.: Belle Grove Publishing, 1994), 172.

9. Survivors Association, *History of the Corn Exchange Regiment*, 672–673, 729.

10. Styple, *With A Flash of His Sword*, 173.

11. Survivors Association, *History of the Corn Exchange Regiment*, 673.

12. Ibid., 400.

13. Ibid., 673.

I Am Going To Fall

14. The 155th Regimental Association, *Under the Maltese Cross: Antietam to Appomattox, The Loyal Uprising in Western Pennsylvania 1861–1865* (Pittsburg, Pa.: The 155th Regimental Association, 1910), 261.

15. Ibid., 404.

16. Amos M. Judson, *History of the Eighty-Third Regiment Pennsylvania Volunteers 1861–1865* (Morningside, 1986), 196.

17. The 155th, *Under the Maltese Cross*, 261.

18. Gordon C. Rhea, *The Battles for Spotsylvania Court House and the Road to Yellow Tavern May 7–12, 1864* (Baton Rouge: Louisiana State University Press, 1997), 57.

19. Judson, *History of the Eighty-Third*, 196–198.

20. The 155th, *Under the Maltese Cross*, 269.

21. Ibid., 404.

A Campaign Too Long

22. Bell Irvin Wiley, *The Life of Billy Yank: The Common Soldier of the Union* (Indianapolis: The Bobbs-Merrill Company, 1952), 274.

23. D. P. Marshall, *Company "K" 155th Pa. Volunteers Zouaves* (1888), 150.

24. United States War Department, *A Compilation of the Official Records of the Union and Confederate Armies*, vol. 36, chap. 48, no. 104 Report of Colonel

Alfred L. Pearson, One hundred and fifty-fifth Pennsylvania Infantry, 558. (Cited hereafter as *O.R.* All volumes are Series 1)

25. 155th PA, *Under the Maltese Cross*, 276.

26. Gordon C. Rhea, *To The North Anna River, Grant and Lee May 13–25, 1864* (Baton Rouge: Louisiana State University Press, 2000), 307.

27. 155th PA, *Under the Maltese Cross*, 276.

28. Ibid., 787.

29. Marshall, *Company "K" 155th Pa. Volunteers Zouaves*, 150.

Death Times Three

30. Stephen W. Sears, *To the Gates of Richmond* (New York: Ticknor & Fields, 1992), 85.

31. Newton Martin Curtis, *From Bull Run to Chancellorsville, The Story of the Sixteenth New York Infantry Together With Personal Reminiscences* (New York: G. P. Putnam's Son, 1906), 96–97.

Death Had No Favorites

32. L. W. Minnigh, *Gettysburg: What They Did Here* (Gettysburg: N. A. Meligakes, 1924), 163.

33. Jacob H. Cole, *Under Five Commanders* (Paterson, N.J.: News Printing Company 1906), 193–194.

34. Ezra J. Warner, *Generals in Blue: Lives of the Union Commanders* (Baton Rouge: Louisiana State University Press, 1964), 576.

35. A. M. Gambone, *The Life of General Samuel K. Zook, Another Forgotten Union Hero* (Baltimore: Butternut and Blue, 1996), vi.

36. Warner, *Generals in Blue*, 576–577.

37. Jorgensen, *The Wheatfield*, 8.

38. Gambone, *Zook*, 7–8.

39. Gilbert Frederick, *The Story of a Regiment Being a Record of the Military Services of the Fifty-Seventh New York State Volunteer Infantry in the War of the Rebellion 1861–1865* (The Fifty-Seventh Veteran Association: 1895), 178–179.

40. *Memorial to Samuel K. Zook* (Philadelphia, Pa.: James Beale Printer, 1889), 17.

41. Gambone, *Zook*, 21–24.

42. *Memorial to Samuel K. Zook*, 17.

43. Gambone, *Zook*, 21–25.

Black Is the Color of the Day

44. Robert Laird Stewart, *History of the One Hundred and Fortieth Regiment Pennsylvania Volunteers* (Philadelphia: Regimental Association, 1912), 102.

45. Charles A. Hale, "With Colonel Cross At the Wheatfield," *Civil War Times Illustrated* (August 1974), 32.

46. Charles A. Fuller, *Personal Recollections of the War of 1861* (Sherburne, N.Y.: New Job Printing House, 1906), 93.

47. Hale, *CWTI*, 34–35.

48. Gregory A. Coco, *Killed in Action* (Gettysburg, Thomas Publications, 1992), 65.

49. Hale, *CWTI*, 36.

50. Coco, *Killed in Action*, 63.

51. Ibid., 62.

52. Stewart, *History of the One Hundred and Fortieth Regiment Pennsylvania Volunteers*, 103.

Death in the Wheatfield

53. Muffly, *The Story of Our Regiment*, 577.

54. Ibid., 569.

55. Ibid., 95–96.

56. Samuel P. Bates, *History of the Pennsylvania Volunteers 1861–5*, 5 vols. (Harrisburg, Pa.: B. Singerly, 1870), IV, 577.

57. Muffly, *The Story of Our Regiment*, 575–576.

58. Ibid., 602.

59. Ibid., 876–877.

60. Ibid., 603.

61. Ibid., 780.

Chapter Three
Coincidences

A Meeting of the Irish

1. Rufus R. Dawes, *Service with the Sixth Wisconsin Volunteers* (Marietta, Ohio: E. R. Alderman & Sons, 1890), 313.

2. Philip Cheek and Mair Pointon, *History of the Sauk County Rifleman, Known as Company "A," Sixth Wisconsin Veteran Volunteer Infantry, 1861–1865* (Madison: Democrat Printing Company, 1909), 49.

3. Ibid., 210.

4. Ibid., 49.

A Knapsack's Return

5. James Madison Stone, *Personal Recollections of the Civil War* (Boston: The Author, 1918), 91–92.

Met Bullets

6. Mrs. Roger A. Pryor, *Reminiscences of Peace and War* (New York: The Macmillan Company, 1904), 395–396.

A Message Delivered

7. R. H. Dudley, "Strange Coincidence in the Army," *Confederate Veteran* (Feb. 1892), 61.

Meeting at the Hornet's Nest

8. Time Life, David Nevin and the Editors of Time-Life Books, *The Road To Shiloh, Early Battles Of The West* (Alexandria: Time Life Books, 1983), 130–131.

9. James Lee McDonough, *Shiloh, In Hell Before Night* (Knoxville: The University of Tennessee Press, 1977), 133–134.

10. Botkin, *A Civil War Treasury of Tales, Legends, and Folklore*, 573–574.

With A Leg Between Them

11. Weymouth T. Jordan, Jr. comp., *North Carolina Troops 1861–1865, A Roster* (Raleigh, 1975), V, 298, 308.

12. J. P. Cannon, "Singular Experience of Brothers," *Confederate Veteran*, II (1896), 385.

A Penny Carved

13. Wiley, *Johnny Reb*, 170; Wiley, *Billy Yank*, 179.

14. Michael Sanders, *Strange Tales of the Civil War* (Shippensburg, Pa.: Burd Street Press, 2001).

15. William J. Wray, *History of the Twenty-Third Pennsylvania Volunteer Infantry, Birney's Zouaves, Three Months and Three Years Service, Civil War 1861–1865* (Philadelphia: Survivors Association Twenty Third Regiment, 1904), 154–155.

Not So Dead After All

16. Dawes, *Service with the Sixth Wisconsin*, 88–89.

17. *O.R.*, vol. 19, chap. 31, no. 25, Report of Lieutenant Colonel Edward S. Bragg, Sixth Wisconsin Infantry of the Battles of South Mountain and Antietam, 255.

18. Warner, *Generals in Blue*, 42.

19. Dawes, *Service with the Sixth Wisconsin*, 99.

A Tribute to Grant

20. King and Derby, *Camp-Fire Sketches*, 59.

21. Warner, *Generals in Blue*, 186.

22. King and Derby, *Camp-Fire Sketches*, 59.

Chapter Four

Ironies

An Odd Name for a Battle

1. Mark Mayo Boatner III, *The Civil War Dictionary* (New York: David McKay Company Inc., 1959), 757.

2. McDonough, *Shiloh*, 213.

3. Ibid., 4.

If the Name Fits, Fight

4. Boatner, *Civil War Dictionary*, 152.

5. Glenn Tucker, *Chickamauga, Bloody Battle in the West* (Dayton: Morningside Bookshop, 1984), 122.

A Grave Situation

6. John R. McBride, *History of the Thirty-Third Indiana Veteran Volunteer Infantry* (Indianapolis: Wm. B. Burford, 1900), 27–28.

7. McBride, *Thirty-Third Indiana*, 220–221.

Orders His Own Execution

8. Michigan Legislature, *Record of Service of Michigan Volunteers in the Civil War 1861–1865* (Kalamazoo: Ihling Bros. and Everard Printers, 1900), 124.

9. Frank Moore, ed. *The Civil War in Song and Story 1860–1865* (New York: P. F. Collier, 1889), 442.

No Guns Allowed

10. William Frassanito, *Early Photography at Gettysburg* (Gettysburg: Thomas Publications, 1995), 153.

11. Harry W. Pfanz, *Gettysburg, Culp's Hill and Cemetery Hill* (Chapel Hill: The University of North Carolina Press, 1993), 25.

12. L. VanLoan Naisawald, *Grape & Canister, The Story of the Field Artillery of the Army of the Potomac, 1861–1865* (Mechanicsburg, Pa.: Stackpole Books, 1999), 288.

13. David G. Martin, *Gettysburg, July 1* (Conshohocken: Combined Books, 1996), 476.

14. Gregory A. Coco, *A Strange and Blighted Land, Gettysburg: The Aftermath of a Battle* (Gettysburg: Thomas Publications, 1995), 12.

Chapter Five

Dreams

Fighting in His Sleep

1. Edward O. Lord, *History of the Ninth Regiment New Hampshire Volunteers in the War of the Rebellion* (Concord, N.H.: Republican Press Association, 1895), 36.

2. Ibid., 248.

3. Ibid., 36.

Dreamed of Murder

4. Frederick H. Dyer, *A Compendium of the War of the Rebellion* (New York: Thomas Yoseloff, 1959), III, 1545.

5. F. M. McAdams, *Every-Day Soldier Life, Or A History of the One Hundred and Thirteenth Ohio Volunteer Infantry* (Columbus: C. M. Cott & Co., 1884), 387.

Saw It in His Dream

6. A Committee of the Regiment, *The Story of the Fifty-Fifth Regiment Illinois Volunteer Infantry in the Civil War 1861–1865*, Reprint (Huntington: Blue Acorn Press, 1993), 451–452.

7. Ibid., 192.

8. Ibid., 192–193.

9. Ibid., 451.

10. Ibid., 193.

11. Ibid., 452.

Death Foretold in A Dream

12. Boatner, *Civil War Dictionary*, 313.

13. Lawrence R. Laboda, *From Selma to Appomattox: The History of the Jeff Davis Artillery* (Shippensburg, Pa.: White Mane Publishing Company Inc., 1994), 70–71.

14. John Purifay, "Was This A Coincidence," *Confederate Veteran*, Vol. IX, No. 4, 1901, 167.

15. Laboda, *From Selma to Appomattox*, 71.

16. Purifay, *Confederate Veteran*, 167.

An Amusing Slumber

17. Wray, *History of the Twenty-Third Pennsylvania*, 158.

18. Ibid., 158.

Chapter Six
The Big Guns

A Shot for Hill

1. Robert Underwood Johnson and Clarence Clough Buel, eds. *Battles and Leaders of the Civil War* (New York: The Century Co., 1887), II, 671.

2. Ibid., 599.

3. Ibid., 671.

Landing in His Lap

4. Ibid.

5. James Longstreet, *From Manassas to Appomattox, Memoirs of the Civil War in America*, reprint (New York: Mallard Press, 1991), 255.

Spiked Gun at Gettysburg

6. *O.R.*, vol. 27, chap. 39, no. 267, Report of Captain Hubert Dilger, Battery I, First Ohio Light Artillery, 754.

7. Martin, *July 1*; William Saxton, *A Regiment Remembered, The 157th New York Volunteers* (Cortland, N.Y.: Cortland County Historical Society, 1996), 75.

8. John S. Applegate, *Reminiscences and Letters of George Arrowsmith of New Jersey* (Red Bank, N.J.: John H. Cook Publisher, 1893), 212.

Another Spiked Gun

9. John H. Rhodes, *The History of Battery B, First Regiment Rhode Island Light Artillery in the War to Preserve the Union 1861–1865* (Providence: Snow & Farnham, 1894), 209.

10. Francis A. Walker, *History of the Second Army Corps*, reprint (Gaithersburg, Md.: Butternut Press, Inc., 1985), 292.

11. Rhodes, *History of Battery B*, 209–210.

12. United States, *Battery B First R.I. Light Artillery, August 13, 1865*, June 12, 1865.

Log Mortars

13. Longstreet, *From Manassas to Appomattox*, 60.

14. E. B. Long, *The Civil War Day By Day, An Almanac 1861–1865* (Garden City: Doubleday & Company, Inc., 1971), 354, 378.

15. Johnson and Buel, *Battles and Leaders*, III, 522.

16. *O.R.*, vol. 24, chap. 36, no. 5, Report of Captain Frederick E. Prime and Cyrus B. Comstock U.S. Corps of Engineers, Chief Engineers Army of the Tennessee, 173.

Justice Is Served

17. King and Derby, *Camp-Fire Sketches*, 85.

Chapter Seven

Dumb Luck

Freak Accidents Happen

1. Albert Lawson, *War Anecdotes and Incidents of Army Life* (Cincinnati: Albert Lawson, 1888), 108–109.

Odd Sense of Timing

2. Survivors Association, *History of the Corn Exchange Regiment*, 369.

3. Ibid., 372.

4. Ibid., 372.

A Lucky Chaplain

5. Ibid., 369, 652.

Saved by the Good Book

6. Mark G. Penrose, *Red: White: and Blue Badge, Pennsylvania Veteran Volunteers. A History of the 93rd Regiment* (Baltimore: Butternut and Blue, 1911), 129–130.

7. George H. Uhler, *Camps and Campaign of the 93d Regiment Penna Vols.,* July 13, 1898.

8. Penrose, *Red: White: and Blue Badge*, 361.

Almost Lost His Head

9. Lord, *History of the Ninth Regiment New Hampshire Volunteers*, 130.

The Keys to Survival

10. Fuller, *Personal Recollections of the War of 1861*, 99.

11. Ibid., 1027.

Rude Awakening

12. John E. Divine, *8th Virginia Infantry.*

13. J. G. De Roulhac Hamilton, ed. *The Papers of Randolph Abbott Shotwell* (Raleigh: the North Carolina Historical Commission, 1931), 95–96.

14. Divine, *8th Virginia*, 80.

Gordon's Rough Day at Antietam

15. Ezra J. Warner, *Generals in Gray, Lives of the Confederate Commanders* (Baton Rouge: Louisiana State University Press, 1959), 111.

16. John B. Gordon, *Reminiscences of the Civil War* (New York: Charles Scribner's Sons, 1905), 84.

17. Ibid., 88.

18. Ibid., 90.

19. Warner, *Generals in Gray*, 111.

Artillery for Supper

20. John L. Parker, *History of the Twenty-Second Massachusetts Infantry, The Second Company Sharpshooters and the Third Light Battery in the War of the Rebellion* (Boston: Regimental Association, 1887), 482.

Blanket Protection

21. Dawes, *Service with the Sixth Wisconsin Volunteers*, 94.

Good Advice

22. Muffly, *The Story of Our Regiment*, 712–713.

23. Ibid., 708.

24. Ibid., 717–718.

25. Ibid., 713–714.

26. Ibid., 990.

Pencils Aren't Just for Writing

27. Ibid., 921.

28. Samuel P. Bates, *History of Pennsylvania Volunteers, 1861–65* (Harrisburg: B. Singerly, 1869), IV, 577.

29. Muffly, *The Story of Our Regiment*, 83–85.

Chapter Eight
Civil War Medicine

A Probing Wound

1. Almira Hancock, *Reminiscences of Winfield Scott Hancock* (New York: Charles L. Webster & Company, 1887), 215.

2. Ibid., 97.

3. A. M. Gambone, *Hancock at Gettysburg ...and beyond* (Baltimore: Butternut and Blue, 1997), 165.

4. Hancock, *Reminiscences of Winfield Scott Hancock*, 97.

5. Gambone, *Hancock at Gettysburg*, 166.

6. Hancock, *Reminiscences of Winfield Scott Hancock*, 99.

7. Gambone, *Hancock at Gettysburg*, 168–170.

8. Ibid., 183.

The Look of Death

9. Musgrove, *Autobiography of Richard W. Musgrove*, 94.

10. J. D. Bloodgood, *Personal Reminiscences of the War* (New York: Hunt & Eaton, 1893), 149–150.

A Hair-raising Incident

11. *The Story of A Bullet*, Grand Army Scout and Soldiers Mail, IV, 1885, 2.

Coughing Bullets

12. Robert J. Driver Jr., *1st Virginia Cavalry* (Lynchburg: H. E. Howard, Inc., 1991).

13. "Strange History of A Bullet," *Confederate Veteran*, Vol. VII, (1899), 169.

How to Be Relieved from Duty

14. Robertson, *Soldiers Blue and Gray*, 217.

15. Billings, *Hardtack and Coffee*, 100.

16. Wiley, *The Life of Billy Yank*, 86.

17. Alfred Jay Ballet, *Civil War Medicine, Challenges and Triumphs* (Tucson: Galen Press, Ltd, 2002), 319.

Left for Dead

18. Massachusetts Adjutant General, Massachusetts *Soldiers, Sailors, and Marines* (Norwood: Norwood Press, 1932), III, 47.

19. *O.R.*, Vol. 36, Chap. 48, no. 265, Report of Colonel Josiah Pickett, Twenty-fifth Massachusetts Infantry, 1016.

20. Frank Moore, ed., *The Civil War in Song and Story* (New York: P. F. Collier, 1889), 487.

21. J. Waldo Denny, *Wearing the Blue in the Twenty-Fifth Mass. Volunteer Infantry with Burnside's Coast Division 18th Army Corps, and the Army of the James* (Worchester: Putnam and Davis, 1879), 326.

22. Massachusetts Adjutant General, *Massachusetts Soldiers, Sailors, and Marines*, III, 47.

Chapter Nine

Tempting Fate

To Be Buried in Such a Beautiful Spot

1. James Lee McDonough and Thomas Connelly, *Five Tragic Hours: The Battle of Franklin* (Knoxville: The University of Tennessee Press, 1983), 35.

2. Warner, *Generals in Gray*, 53–54.

3. McDonough and Connelly, *Five Tragic Hours*, 35.

4. J. B. Hood, *Advance and Retreat, The Autobiography of General J. B. Hood*, reprint (New York: Konecky and Konecky, n.d.), 294.

5. Howell Purdue and Elizabeth Purdue, *Pat Cleburne Confederate General* (Hillsboro, Tex.: Hill Jr. College Press, 1973), 421–423.

6. McDonough and Connelly, *Five Tragic Hours*, 160.

7. Ibid., 167.

8. Ibid., 35.

To Die in Old Pennsylvania

9. Judson, *History of the Eighty-Third*, 123.

10. Oliver Wilcox Norton, *The Attack and Defense of Little Round Top, Gettysburg, July 2, 1863*, reprint (New York: Konecky & Konecky, 1913), 285.

11. Warner, *Generals in Blue*, 527–528.

12. Judson, *History of the Eighty-Third*, 138–140.

The Bullet Is Not Moulded

13. Applegate, *Reminiscences and Letters of George Arrowsmith of New Jersey*, 211.

14. Ibid., 21.

15. Ibid., 143.

16. Ibid., 163.

17. Ibid., 143.

18. Ibid., 210–212.

19. Martin, *Gettysburg, July 1*, 301–302; Applegate, *Letters of George Arrowsmith*, 214.

20. Saxton, *A Regiment Remembered*, 76.

21. Applegate, *Letters of George Arrowsmith*, 215–217.

22. Martin, *Gettysburg, July 1*, 302.

Almost Too Self-Assured

23. John Anderson, *The Fifty-Seventh Regiment of Massachusetts Volunteers in the War of the Rebellion* (Boston: E. A. Stillings & Co., 1896), 122–123.

Bibliography

Books

Anderson, John. *The Fifty-Seventh Regiment of Massachusetts Volunteers in the War of the Rebellion*. Boston: E. A. Stillings & Co., 1896.

Applegate, John S. *Reminiscences and Letters of George Arrowsmith of New Jersey*. Red Bank, N.J.: John H. Cook Publisher, 1893.

Ballet, Alfred Jay. *Civil War Medicine, Challenges and Triumphs*. Tucson: Galen Press, Ltd., 2002.

Bates, Samuel P. *History of Pennsylvania Volunteers, 1861–65*. 5 vols. Harrisburg, Pa.: B. Singerly, 1870.

Billings, John D. *Hardtack and Coffee or The Unwritten Story of Army Life*. Gettysburg: Civil War Times Illustrated (Reprint), 1974.

Bloodgood, J. D. *Personal Reminiscences of the War*. New York: Hunt & Eaton, 1893.

Boatner, Mark Mayo III. *The Civil War Dictionary*. New York: David McKay Company, Inc., 1959.

Botkin B. A., ed., *A Civil War Treasury of Tales, Legends, and Folklore.* New York: Promontory Press, 1960.

Cheek, Philip, and Mair Pointon. *History of the Sauk County Riflemen, Known as Company "A," Sixth Wisconsin Volunteer Infantry, 1861–1865.* Democrat Printing Company: Madison, 1909.

Coco, Gregory A. *A Strange and Blighted Land, Gettysburg, The Aftermath of a Battle.* Gettysburg: Thomas Publications, 1995.

———. *Killed in Action.* Gettysburg: Thomas Publications, 1992.

Cole, Jacob H. *Under Five Commanders.* Paterson, N.J.: News Printing Company, 1906.

Commager, Henry Steele. *The Blue and the Gray*, reprint. New York: The Fairfax Press, 1982.

A Committee of the Regiment. *The Story of the Fifty-Fifth Regiment Illinois Volunteer Infantry in the Civil War 1861–1865*, reprint. Huntington, W. Va.: Blue Acorn Press, 1993.

Curtis, Newton Martin. *From Bull Run to Chancellorsville: The Story of the Sixteenth New York Infantry Together With Personal Reminiscences.* New York: G. P. Putnam's Son, 1906.

Dawes, Rufus R. *Service with the Sixth Wisconsin Volunteers.* Marietta, Ohio: E. R. Alderman & Sons, 1890.

Denny, J. Waldo. *Wearing the Blue in the Twenty-Fifth Mass. Volunteer Infantry With Burnside's Coast Division 18th Army Corps, and the Army of the James.* Worcester: Putnam and Davis, 1879.

Driver, Robert J. Jr. *1st Virginia Cavalry.* Lynchburg: H. E. Howard, Inc., 1991.

Dyer, Frederick H. *A Compendium of the War of the Rebellion.* New York: Thomas Yoseloff, 1959.

Frassanito, William. *Early Photography at Gettysburg.* Gettysburg: Thomas Publications, 1995.

Frederick, Gilbert. *The Story of a Regiment Being a Record of the Military Services of the Fifty-Seventh Volunteer Infantry in the War of the Rebellion 1861–1865.* Chicago, Ill.: The Fifty-Seventh Veteran Association, 1895.

Fuller, Charles A. *Personal Recollections of the War of 1861.* Sherburne, N.Y.: New Job Printing House, 1906.

Gambone, A. M. *Hancock at Gettysburg... and beyond.* Baltimore: Butternut and Blue, 1997.

————. *The Life of General Samuel K. Zook, Another Forgotten Union Hero.* Baltimore: Butternut and Blue, 1996.

Gordon, John B. *Reminiscences of the Civil War.* New York: Charles Scribner's Sons, 1905.

Hamilton, J. G. De Roulhac, ed. *The Papers of Randolph Abbott Shotwell.* Raleigh: North Carolina Historical Commission, 1931.

Hancock, Almira. *Reminiscences of Winfield Scott Hancock.* New York: Charles L.Webster & Company, 1887.

Hood, J. B. *Advance and Retreat. The Autobiography of General J. B. Hood,* reprint. New York: Konecky and Konecky, n.d.

Johnson, Robert Underwood, and Clarence Clough Buel, eds. *Battles and Leaders of the Civil War.* New York: The Century Co., 1887.

Jordan, Weymouth T. Jr. *North Carolina Troops 1861–1865, A Roster.* Raleigh: 1975.

Jorgensen, Jay. *The Wheatfield at Gettysburg: A Walking Tour.* Gettysburg: Thomas Publications, 2002.

Judson, Amos M. *History of the Eighty-Third Regiment Pennsylvania Volunteers 1861–1865,* reprint. Dayton, Ohio: Morningside, 1986.

Keesy, Rev. W. A. *War as Viewed From the Ranks.* Norwalk: The Experiment and News Co., 1898.

King, W. C., and W. P. Derby, comps. *Camp-Fire Sketches and Battle-Field Echoes.* Springfield, Mass.: King, Richardson & Co., 1888.

Laboda, Lawrence R. *From Selma to Appomattox: The History of the Jeff Davis Artillery.* Shippensburg, Pa.: White Mane Publishing, 1994.

Lawson, Albert. *War Anecdotes and Incidents of Army Life.* Cincinnati: Albert Lawson, 1888.

Lippy, John D. Jr. *The War Dog.* Harrisburg, Pa.: Telegraph Press, 1962.

Long, E. B. *The Civil War Day by Day, An Almanac 1861–1865.* Garden City: Doubleday & Company, Inc., 1971.

Longstreet, James. *From Manassas to Appomattox, Memoirs of the Civil War in America,* reprint. New York: Mallard Press, 1991.

Lord, Edward O. *History of the Ninth Regiment New Hampshire Volunteers in the War of the Rebellion.* Concord, N.H.: Republican Press Association, 1895.

Marshall, D. P. *Company "K" 155th Pa. Volunteers Zouaves,* n.p., 1888.

Martin, David G. *Gettysburg, July 1*. Revised ed. Conshohocken, Pa.: Combined Books, 1996.

Massachusetts Adjutant General. *Massachusetts Soldiers, Sailors, and Marines*. Norwood, Mass.: Norwood Press, 1932.

McAdams, F. M. *Every-Day Soldier Life, Or a History of the One Hundred and Thirteenth Ohio Volunteer Infantry*. Columbus: C. M. Cott & Co., printers, 1884.

McBride, John R. *History of the Thirty-Third Indiana Veteran Volunteer Infantry*. Indianapolis: Wm. B. Burford, 1900.

McDonough, James Lee. *Shiloh, In Hell Before Night*. Knoxville: The University of Tennessee Press, 1977.

McDonough, James Lee, and Thomas Connelly. *Five Tragic Hours, The Battle of Franklin*. Knoxville: The University of Tennessee Press, 1983.

Michigan Legislature. *Record of Service of Michigan Volunteers in the Civil War, 1861–1865*. Kalamazoo: Ihling Bros. & Everard, printers, 1900.

Minnigh, L. W. *Gettysburg: What They Did Here*. Gettysburg: N. A. Meligakes, 1924.

Moore, Frank, ed. *The Civil War in Song and Story 1860–1865*. New York: P. F. Collier, 1889.

Muffly, J. W. *The Story of Our Regiment: A History of the 148th Pennsylvania Volunteers*. Des Moines: Kenyon Printing & Mfg. Co., 1904.

Mulholland, St. Clair. *The Story of the 116th Regiment Pennsylvania Volunteers in the War of the Rebellion*. Philadelphia: F. McManus, Jr. & Co., 1903.

Musgrove, Richard W. *Autobiography of Capt. Richard W. Musgrove*. Mary D. Musgrove, 1921.

Naisawald, L. VanLoan. *Grape & Canister: The Story of the Field Artillery of the Army of the Potomac, 1861–1865.* Mechanicsburg, Pa.: Stackpole Books, 1999.

Norton, Oliver Wilcox. *The Attack and Defense of Little Round Top, Gettysburg, July 2, 1863*, reprint. New York: Konecky & Konecky, 1913.

The 155th Regimental Association. *Under the Maltese Cross, Antietam to Appomattox, The Loyal Uprising in Western Pennsylvania 1861–1865.* Pittsburg, Pa.: The 155th Regimental Association, 1910.

Parker, John L. *History of the Twenty-Second Massachusetts Infantry, The Second Company Sharpshooters and the Third Light Battery in the War of the Rebellion.* Boston: Regimental Association, 1887.

Patterson, Gerard A. *Debris of Battle: The Wounded of Gettysburg.* Mechanicsburg, Pa.: Stackpole Books, 1997.

Pember, Phoebe Yates. *A Southern Woman's Story: Life in Confederate Richmond.* Wilmington, N.C.: Broadfoot Publishing, 1991.

Penrose, Mark G. *Red: White: and Blue Badge, Pennsylvania Veteran Volunteers, A History of the 93rd Regiment*, reprint. Baltimore: Butternut and Blue, 1911.

Pfanz, Harry W. *Gettysburg, Culp's Hill and Cemetery Hill.* Chapel Hill: The University of North Carolina Press, 1993.

———. *Gettysburg, The Second Day.* Chapel Hill: The University of North Carolina Press, 1987.

Priest, John Michael. *Nowhere to Run, The Wilderness, May 4th & 5th, 1864.* Shippensburg: White Mane Publishing, 1995.

Pryor, Mrs. Roger A. *Reminiscences of Peace and War.* New York: The Macmillan Company, 1904.

Purdue, Howell, and Elizabeth Purdue. *Pat Cleburne Confederate General.* Hillsboro, Tex.: Hill Jr. College Press, 1973.

Rhea, Gordon C. *The Battles for Spotsylvania Court House and the Road to Yellow Tavern May 7–12, 1864.* Baton Rouge: Louisiana State University Press, 1997.

———. *To the North Anna River, Grant and Lee May 13–25, 1864.* Baton Rouge: Louisiana State University Press, 2000.

Rhodes, John H. *The History of Battery B, First Regiment Rhode Island Light Artillery in the War to Preserve the Union 1861–1865.* Providence: Snow & Farnham, 1894.

Robertson, James F. Jr. *Soldiers Blue and Gray.* Columbia: University of South Carolina, 1988.

Sanders, Michael. *Strange Tales of the Civil War.* Shippensburg, Pa.: Burd Street Press, 2001.

Saxton, William. *A Regiment Remembered, The 157th New York Volunteers.* Cortland, N.Y.: Cortland County Historical Society, 1996.

Sears, Stephen W. *To the Gates of Richmond.* New York: Ticknor & Fields, 1992.

Soley, James Russell. *The Navy in the Civil War: The Blockade and the Cruisers.* New York: Charles Scribner's Sons, 1883.

Stewart, Robert Laird. *History of the One Hundred and Fortieth Regiment Pennsylvania Volunteers.* Philadelphia, Pa.: Regimental Association, 1912.

Stone, James Madison. *Personal Recollections of the Civil War.* Boston: The Author, 1918.

Styple, William B., ed. *With A Flash of His Sword: The Writings of Major Holman S. Melcher 20th Maine Infantry.* Kearny, N.J.: Belle Grove Publishing, 1994.

Survivors Association of the 118th (Corn Exchange) Regiment P. V. *History of the Corn Exchange Regiment 118th Pennsylvania Volunteers.* Philadelphia: J. L. Smith, 1888.

Time Life Books, David Nevin, ed. 27 vols. *The Road to Shiloh, Early Battles of the West,* Alexandria: Time Life Books, 1983.

Tucker, Glenn. *Chickamauga, Bloody Battle in the West.* Dayton: Morningside Bookshop, 1984.

United States, *Battery B First R.I. Light Artillery, August 13, 1865–June 12, 1865.*

United States War Department. *A Compilation of the Official Records of the Union and Confederate Armies.* 128 Vols. Washington, D.C., 1880–91.

Walker, Francis A. *History of the Second Army Corps,* reprint. Gaithersburg, Md.: Butternut Press, 1895.

Warner, Ezra J. *Generals in Blue: Lives of the Union Commanders.* Baton Rouge: Louisiana State University Press, 1964.

———. *Generals in Gray: Lives of the Confederate Commanders.* Baton Rouge: Louisiana State University Press, 1959.

Wash, W. A. *Camp, Field, and Prison Life.* Saint Louis: Southwestern Book and Publishing Co., 1870.

Wiley, Bell Irvin, *The Life of Billy Yank, The Common Soldier of the Union.* Indianapolis: The Bobbs-Merrill Company, 1952.

———. *The Life of Johnny Reb: The Common Soldier of the Confederacy.* Indianapolis: The Bobbs-Merrill Company, 1943.

Wray, William J. *History of the Twenty-Third Pennsylvania Volunteer Infantry, Birney's Zouaves, Three Months and Three Years Service, Civil War 1861–1865.* Philadelphia: Survivors Association Twenty-Third Regiment, 1904.

Periodicals

The Bivouac. Boston: Bivouac Publishing Company, 1885.

Blue & Gray, Fall 1997.

Camps and Campaigns of the 93rd Regiment Penna. Vols.

Civil War Times Illustrated, August 1974.

Confederate Veteran, Feb. 1892.

Confederate Veteran, II, 1896.

Confederate Veteran, VII, 1899.

Confederate Veteran, Vol. IX, No. 4, 1901.

Confederate Veteran, Vol. XVII, No. 7, July 1909.

Grand Army Scout and Soldiers Mail, IV, 1899.

Index